6-28-22

CALLED
BY NAME

Robert J. Furey

CALLED BY NAME

Discovering your unique purpose in life

A Crossroad Book
The Crossroad Publishing Company
New York

This printing: 2000

The Crossroad Publishing Company
370 Lexington Avenue, New York, NY 10017

Printed in the United States of America

Furey, Robert J.
    Called by name : discovering your unique purpose in life / Robert J. Furey.
        p.   cm.
    ISBN 0-8245-1484-X (pbk.)
    1. Vocation.   I. Title.
BL629.F87   1995
291.4–dc20   94–49055
                                                         CIP

To my son Daniel.
And to the memory and spirit
of Katherine Maureen.

Contents

Introduction

This book began with a small seed planted somewhere along the line. I had first heard the notion that people have callings sent by God back when I was a child. It sounded so outlandish, though, that it was easy to dismiss as foolishness. Then in recent years that small seed began to sprout the question *What if?*

What if people really are called to certain tasks? What if all those self-help books are wrong about how we are in complete control of our destinies? What if each and every one of us has his or her own mission (or set of missions) and right path in life? What if we have callings but miss them? What if we miss them because we never listened hard enough?

As time passed, curiosity evolved into conviction. I came to believe in callings. Furthermore, I've come to believe now that *everyone* has a calling. Everyone is called to fulfill a purpose. We can choose to turn away from our callings, but there are (as we shall see) consequences for this. We will also examine the rewards for following the way that has been given to each of us.

This book does not remove all the mysteries of callings. Specifically, there are two important questions that I cannot answer for you. First, who/what/where is the source of your calling? I can answer this only for me. I will suggest, however, that you will find the source of your calling only by *answering* your calling. And as you near the source, its image may change. So your answer depends on where you are on your path. Hopefully, you will come close enough to the source to know it.

There is then a second fundamental question: Why have you been called to do your particular work? This one may never be answered. I have considered a variety of explanations, but I keep coming back to the same place — I don't know. I don't know why you were given your unique calling and why I was given mine. I can accept that we are each given work that needs to be done. It's how the work gets distributed that puzzles me.

Callings may also be referred to as missions or visions. Some people will associate the idea with the religious notion of vocation. We begin, then, with a discussion of the meaning of callings. We will look at the evidence that points to their existence and will then consider the consequences of missing your callings as well as your rewards for following them. Finally, we will look at ways to connect with your callings.

The material presented in this book comes from a number of sources. While most people may consider the calling a theological concept, I have not used theology as my primary reference. In an effort to generate new thought and discussion on this topic, I have gathered material from other fields, such as psychology, philosophy, literature, medicine, anthropology, management studies, political science, biology, and history. Clearly, a purely theological discussion is, at best, incomplete.

A word of caution. Any writer who dares to call his or her work "nonfiction" must proceed with an ample dose of humility. What follows is an explanation of the nature of callings. It does not presume to be *the* explanation. I have tried to put the pieces together in a reasonable manner. I have tried to present the most likely conclusions based on the evidence at hand. But I would prefer to think of this work as an introduction rather than a conclusion. Let it invite reflection and discussion. The final word belongs to you and to the One who calls you by name.

Chapter One

Callings

Man is asked to make of himself what he is supposed to become to fulfill his destiny.

— PAUL TILLICH

Every blade of grass has its Angel that bends over it and whispers, "Grow, grow."

— THE TALMUD

Belief in callings has been around for thousands of years. And the skepticism, I suppose, has been around just as long.

There is nothing new in the idea that we each have our own unique callings that urge us to move in specific directions. And, like most things, where there are believers there are nonbelievers. For many of us, there comes a time in life when we have to make a choice. Do I have a calling or do I not? Unfortunately, many souls run out of life before they settle this, before they realize they have a calling all their own, before they realize what it is.

Certain cultures have suggested that only a select few are given callings, callings being a privilege of royalty or the clergy alone. This notion may not pertain to us directly, but it does lead to the particularly thorny issue of the source of callings. A calling might appear to be a spiritual phenomenon, inevitably linked to God. Yet atheists have asserted that callings are also consistent with their atheism. And even if we could agree that a calling is the voice of God, we must still ask: Who or what is God to you?

It is most intriguing to realize how *little* has been said about callings in recent years. The phenomenon that may be the most powerful force in determining the course of our lives has been virtually left out of contemporary thought. The idea has been belittled and avoided. At most we speak of how it seems "as if" people "might" be called to make their own singular contributions.

I begin now by suggesting that *all* people have callings. Everyone. We are all on earth with special duties. No exceptions. You are here for a reason, a very important reason. You have neither the right nor the power to have someone else make your contributions. If you do not live out your calling, that calling will go forever unanswered. Then, a singular, crucial force in the development and improvement of humankind will be lost.

Russian poet Osip Mandelstam, who died in one of Stalin's prisons, wrote, "You must live out your whole life in order to realize that it doesn't belong to you." Mandelstam knew that our destiny is not completely our own creation. We are each here to discover our own mission. The first step to learning the nature of this mission is to understand that it exists. Once we accept the reality of a calling, we can focus on responding to it. In other words, you may have to believe it to see it; you may have to take a leap of faith before your path itself materializes. Once you begin to believe, your direction will emerge.

In 1927, the genius Buckminster Fuller was on the verge of suicide. Before he could carry out this act, however, he heard a voice say, "You do not have the right to eliminate yourself. You do not belong to you. You belong to the universe."[1] Fuller opted for life and went on to a brilliant career making his very important mark upon the world.

Your mission, or set of missions, in life is more than just a job or a career. Answering a call means more than deciding to be a doctor, a lawyer, or a street musician. You can quit a job. You can retire from a career. But you cannot divorce yourself from your calling. Even if you refuse to acknowledge it, it's there. You cannot amputate your soul. You are called to make a life for yourself that allows you to contribute what you alone can do. You are not merely called to a job; you are called to a life. And you impact the universe in ways known more by who you are than by what you do.

In 1992 at the Republican National Convention, in his speech accepting his party's nomination, President George Bush said, "There comes a time when God introduces you to yourself." This is the time when we begin to comprehend our purpose in life. Some of us are introduced early in life while others meet themselves much later on. Something about this monumental introduction requires that the time be right.

Before we go any further, though, we need to return to the issue of the calling's origin. Where does a calling begin? Many, like Mr. Bush, have asserted that the voice belongs to God. Others have contended that we are called from within by entities such as the "inner self" or the unconscious. Still others have insisted that our biological makeup prepares us, indeed drives us, toward certain destinations. The answer is, to say the least, debatable.

I won't try to settle the issue. As important as this question is, it cannot be answered by anyone but you. Meeting the voice that calls you will occur only as you respond to it. No one can tell you who or what is calling you. You have to describe it to yourself.

Take, for instance, the case of Carl Jung. One of the most influential psychiatrists who ever lived, Jung spent most of his career teaching that we all have a guide that lives within us: the unconscious. He said that if we listen to the voice of our unconscious, we will be led to our purpose in life. He felt that the unconscious was most often heard through dreams, symbols, art, and meditation. If we develop an ear for our unconscious, we will come to know our place in the universe.

Shortly before his death, however, Jung added a tremendously important dimension to his work. He acknowledged the existence of God. The unconscious for him hence became more a place where information is stored or communicated and less a *source* of wisdom and guidance. During his last months, Jung came to believe that God speaks to us through our unconscious. The unconscious, then, is the mail carrier, not the sender.

We can only hypothesize, but it may have been that during the course of his life Jung followed his unconscious as far as it could take him. Having reached the end of that trail, he found what he believed to be God. Although during most of his life he believed that we are guided by our unconscious, he died with the conviction that he had found God to be his Caller. His calling led him to the point where he saw its origin.

Even if Jung *began* his life's mission with a commitment to a belief in God, finding God at the end of his work might still have been a revelation. The God you find by answering your call may be quite different from the one you were taught about. It may be a more powerful, loving, and personal God. It may be a God who has a special interest in you rather than an abstract God who lives far away beyond the clouds. But, as I said, no one can answer this for you. You must follow your calling in order to comprehend the true nature of the One who calls.

Maybe hearing the words of others will help illuminate the meaning of a calling. "God, our Lord, distinguishes each one of us from all the others," said Polish leader and Nobel Peace Prize winner Lech Walesa. "He assigned a task for every person."[2] This "task" is, I believe, what Howard Thurman meant when he advised that we "listen for the sound of the genuine" in ourselves. "It is the only true guide we will ever have. And if you cannot hear it, you will all of your life spend your days on the ends of strings that somebody else pulls."[3]

Psychotherapist and philosopher Sheldon Kopp expressed a similar sentiment:

> Within each one of us there is a pearl of great value. It is solely our own and cannot be found in anyone else. If we are to claim our prized uniqueness, without knowing exactly what we are looking for, we must search our souls for directions, and listen to what our hearts have to tell us about how to find this hidden treasure. This precious pearl that is our individual worth can only be found when we are willing to stand alone.[4]

Walesa, Thurman, and Kopp believe that individuality and uniqueness are essential to finding your task, your sound of the genuine, your pearl. It's not something you can find in someone else's book. It's something you must find for yourself, by yourself.

This is not a tragic situation. Rather, the prospect of going through this process should foster optimism. I like to believe that most people eventually find their true direction, which is due at least in part to the work of those talented people (such as the ones mentioned above) who keep reminding others that we all have a special set of challenges.

Certainly we could focus on the negative. It's there. The aimless wandering. The bitterness. In his book _The Tao of Pooh,_ Benjamin Hoff observes, "Everything has its own place and function. That applies to people, although many don't seem to realize it, stuck as they are in the wrong job, the wrong marriage, or the wrong house. When you know and respect your own Inner Nature, you know where you belong. You also know where you *don't* belong."[5] There lives a certain wisdom in pain. Your pain is capable of saying to you, "You don't belong here. For God's sake, move on! Move in the direction that eases the pain."

In his studies on how to improve one's quality of life, psychologist Mihaly Csikszentmihalyi makes an observation similar to many other researchers before him: "The waiting rooms of psychiatrists are filled with rich and successful patients who, in their forties and fifties, suddenly wake up to the fact that a plush suburban home, expensive cars, and even an Ivy League education are not enough to bring peace of mind."[6] Although some might be quick to call this awakening a tragedy, it most certainly is not. The point where these people "suddenly wake up" is a triumph. A calling cannot be bought. It cannot be manipulated by even the most powerful, intelligent people. It never lets go. Even when an entire culture indicates to you that you have it all, or vice versa, that you have nothing, your message stands strong, belonging only to you. Not only that: you belong to it.

Change very often brings pain; pain likewise can inspire difficult but necessary changes. When pain communicates a need to make changes, the nature of the changes is not at first always clear. If we learn its language, however, pain can be a remarkable teacher. It can help lead us to where we belong.

While I was researching this book, I spent some time studying Native American cultures. I felt certain that the Native Americans would provide important lessons on the events by which people find their way. In the process, I learned that their stories and legends consistently demonstrate a fascinat-

ing dimension. In these tales, *virtually everything has a voice.*
The modern Western worldview tends to accept that only
people and maybe a few animals are empowered to communicate. But in the Native American stories anything and
everything can teach: the clouds, the fire, the wind, the earth,
the sun, the snow, the quiet, the forest, the thunder, and the
lightning. They all have the power of speech. Your ancestors,
your unborn children, the gods, your god, your spirit guide,
your fear, your anger, your disabilities, your love — all speak
your name and your language.

An early exposure to this type of art and literature would
sensitize us to the subtle lessons of the universe. But we have
become so civilized that most of *our* universe is silent. We are
not raised to listen to the breeze or the ponds. And wouldn't
we view taking advice from the ocean as an expression of
some kind of mental illness? The ocean isn't supposed to talk
in a rational world.

So it is with pain. We find it hard to allow it a voice. The
simple question What is your pain saying to you? can be too
threatening for many people to ponder seriously. They cringe
and wonder, "Isn't it crazy to ask that?" The correct answer, of course, is no. It's very healthy to ask your pain for
guidance. Pain can provide you with the direction you lack.

Unfortunately for them, overly civilized people don't realize this. They do not give themselves the freedom to talk to
their hurt or their confusion. They are too "sane" to do so. So
they remain unquestionably sane, and often quite successful,
yet they are terribly lost.

The belief that each human being has a particular set of
tasks and completely unique road to travel is preposterous
to some. A percentage of these skeptics doubt that there
is enough room for everyone to have his or her own purpose and place. Others offer a more biological explanation
of their disbelief. They maintain that the primary objective

of human behavior has always been self-preservation. This group maintains that our single strongest instinct is to protect our existence and that this drive, more than anything else, determines how we live. In other words, we live to keep ourselves alive.

This is an especially dismal outlook. If self-preservation is the primary objective of our lives, then all life ends in failure. Physical life inevitably ends in death. And the value of one's life can never be measured by one's birthdays.

The purpose of our lives involves so much more than simply staying alive. The quality of our lives is more accurately measured by what we do with the life we've been given than by how long we have lived. The theory of self-preservation is attractive because it is so simple and concrete. The idea that our real purpose in life is to answer our callings requires more thought and certainly more patience.

Happily, there is indeed evidence that each of us has a calling, and this evidence is difficult to deny. Callings produce a feeling that really has no name. It can be intriguing or frightening, or it may be immediately exhilarating. The feeling of a calling is quite unique, and it is this uniqueness that calls attention to it. It can begin as a voice of despair or a message from any element of nature. Even when the message cannot be clearly interpreted, a person is left with the sensation, "Something has happened. Something essential has been planted in me." What that "something" is may take time to unfold — or it may blossom in seconds.

Sometimes we have to struggle to be able to hear the message. More often, however, we are not able to *stop* hearing it. Your callings hound you. They don't disappear. The volume may decrease for a time, but the call is still there, in the still, small voice. Your calling may settle you when you are upset, or it may upset you when you are settled. It can be a comfort or a provocation. It may ask you to stop and contemplate, or it may urge you to plunge into action. Only you know. The message is given to you alone.

There is never a need to doubt whether you'll be able to follow your call once you find it. Everyone's calling is attainable no matter how challenging it may be. You have what you need to complete your tasks. No one is spiritually disabled. It may be necessary, of course, to first make an honest appraisal of your gifts and limitations. When you realize the instruments you possess (as well as those you do not), you begin to understand the kind of music you were meant to make. Everyone has his or her own sound, a sound that is somehow necessary not only for us as individuals but also for the world.

A warning: the first calling you feel may not be your final calling. It may only be your next step. Mother Teresa claimed that we could have a "calling within a calling." You may, for instance, feel deeply compelled by and thoroughly interested in growing plants. As a result you may study agriculture in college. After receiving your training, however, you may feel a pull to apply your knowledge in some other field like environmental studies, for example.

The strongest evidence of a calling is what you feel inside. The hard part is that you have to *let yourself* feel it and think about it and see it and hear it. It's not always obvious. It may be hidden beneath all those things people want you to be; or it may be drowned out by the noises made by fear, greed, or the desire to control every aspect of your life.

Finally, before we move on, there is one more basic issue to attend to. The expression "You've missed your calling" has become a more than worn-out cliché in our age. It is used when someone — usually an adult — displays a talent that has not earlier been put to use. As overused as this expression is, it has not been given adequate consideration. The fact is, the phrase is never right: as long as you are alive, so is your calling. The calling never dies. There is no cause to grieve the calling you *missed,* only the one you are *missing.* You may have lost time and opportunity but not your mission. Someone could realize a calling on her or his deathbed. In this case, the tragedy would be having only a short time to walk the given path. The triumph, however, would be that this person could walk that path into the next life.

To say "You missed your calling" makes no sense if it is directed toward a living human being. Callings live along with people. What can be said to someone who has lost course is, "You are *missing* your calling." This is all we can correctly say to ourselves or anyone else. Your true path is always alive. You will never reach a time when you can rightly say to yourself, "It's over." You can waste time and turn away opportunities, but your callings will never leave you.

Resistance

Callings, especially at first, often involve a good deal of uncertainty. What if I'm called to do something I can't do? What if it's something my friends and/or family won't appreciate or approve of? What if what I think is my real calling is not my real calling? What if...?

On your path you will need to walk through fear, sometimes a lot of it. No one has ever traveled your road. You will be tempted to leave your mission for one that has been completed by others, for in so doing you would be able to follow their tracks and avoid their mistakes. You could then leave the pioneering to those who have the courage to be pioneers.

In his essay "Self-Reliance," Ralph Waldo Emerson advises, "Trust thyself. Great men have always done so." Great men — pioneers. Pioneers, great men and women, whatever you call them, all find the courage to trust themselves. This is not to say they feel no fear. They feel the urge to hesitate and procrastinate (both are based in fear), then move in their own special directions.

Everyone feels this fear at some time or another. It's just that some — the pioneers — refuse to let fear make their decisions for them. They know that fear is an obstacle and not an end point. It's something to be passed through. Their drive is much more powerful than their fright. Psychiatrist David Viscott describes this well when he writes, "The greatest courage comes from the highest conviction.... When you have an objective worth risking for, your actions become purposeful and your life begins to make sense.... Your courage to risk comes from the belief that your ideals are worthy."[7] With your cause comes your courage.

Dostoyevsky said that "taking a new step, uttering a new word, is what people fear most." Feeling yourself pulled in a new direction isn't always easy. There are those who feel that this is insanity tugging at them. Besides the newness, there is a certain loss of control, a letting go of the comfortable and predictable while moving into the unknown. In its early stages, a breakthrough can feel like a breakdown.

An old prayer says, "Lord, teach us when to let go." We need to move in the face of uncertainty. We can find guidance on how to know and follow our visions, but this guidance is not in the form of a detailed map. Sometimes it comes in the form of symbols or art. Poetry, for example, may have many interpretations and meanings, but probably only one is quite right for you. Finding this special, personal meaning may take time. Also, your meaning may not become clear until you have made a few mistakes in interpretation.

So it is with a calling. You may be mistaken. There is room for misinterpretation. You may have to "pick yourself up, dust yourself off, then start over again," this time a little wiser. But remember, callings are found by those who are willing to be called — those who are willing to work in harmony with the universe instead of insisting that they dominate and control all that surrounds them. You have to be willing to let go in order to find destiny.

It would be easier if callings were more like instincts. With instincts there are no distractions: one is simply moved by hunger, thirst, and so on. With callings there may be many distractions to confuse and complicate. You could be mistaken. You could be embarrassed. You could run right into any number of the "What ifs...?"

Hearing a call is not always a perfect process: mistakes are sometimes made. But the mistakes, in their own way, can be part of your correct path. One of the most important lessons learned in the process of finding your true calling is to understand that there are no wasted experiences. There are no episodes in the course of your life that are to be placed in exile. Everything that you have lived through, or will ever live through, has a message for you, a message you are to keep — a message that may appear meaningless or too painful to hold but that, after a time, reveals itself as essential to your missions in life; a message that, by itself, may provide little direction but when placed alongside other events in your life may complete the puzzle of who you are meant to be.

Some people are tempted to resign from the search for their true meaning due to a fear of being wrong. Other people resist their callings because they fear what they will find if they are right. They are afraid that their Caller will ask them to be something that is not acceptable to them or to the important people in their lives. They burden themselves with possibilities such as: "If I 'let go,' I could end up having to leave home and be with unfamiliar people, people who are sick or in trouble." This is the fear that one may not be able to accept one's destiny. Then there is the fear of abandonment: "If people knew the *real* me, they would leave me."

These fears are honest and genuine, should be treated with respect, and can serve an important purpose. Callings do not ask for impulsive changes, and fear, in its healthy form, urges us to pause and consider the next step. Fear cautions us to slow down, but it doesn't necessarily mean stop. If we respect it and accept it into our lives, fear can be a marvelous teacher. In the end, fear asks us the same question Hamlet struggled with: "Are you up to your destiny?"

Besides fear, there is another force that leads some people to fight their callings. The existence of a calling suggests that we are not as free as many of us would like to be. If we accept that the path has chosen us, then we must forfeit our illusions of being masters of our destiny. We release some control, and in return we, eventually, receive direction. Yet many do not want to lose the control. They desperately want to choose their paths.

Rollo May made the point that "from the beginning of history...the principle of freedom is considered more precious than life itself."[8] We want to have all the options. Many individuals are convinced that total freedom is our right, that somehow we are entitled to every choice we could possibly envision. In this world without limitations we could be whatever we want. Is it any wonder that growing up can be so difficult? If we are to mature, we must release this illusion of complete freedom. We need to accept that we have limitations and that these limitations, along with our gifts, point us toward our mission.

In order to hear your calling you must be willing to accept that while you can make any choice you like, not all choices will be right for you. All choices are not equal. What we *can* do helps point us in the direction of what we *need* to be doing. Just as our powers are limited, so too are our correct paths. What is right for you may be wrong for everyone else. Erik Erikson believed that one of the most crucial steps in the maturing process came when identification moved toward identity. In brief, this is the point when we understand that we are not our heroes. We begin to understand that we have our own directions. Instead of striving to be someone else, we come to accept the flaws (i.e., limitations) that define us. Then, hopefully, there comes an acceptance of our identity. We may not be able to become our heroes, but neither will they ever be able to become us.

Maybe a useful analogy would be that of a man who is traveling without any clear destination. He can choose any road he wishes. He can go north or south, east or west. He can travel aimlessly in all directions. The problem is that he might just go long and far and see and do many exhilarating things without recognizing that he is not where he should be. Eventually, when reality breaks through his denial and he realizes that the road he has taken (though enchanting at first) leads nowhere, he faces a crisis. The traveler who moves without guidance is likely to find himself lost. Someday, he may even find himself lost and feeling paralyzed.

I recently read the results of a survey that asked people what they had learned in life. One insightful sixty-three-year-old answered: "I've learned that people who have mastered the art of living seem to be guided by an internal compass. They may not always stay on track, but they have a way of always returning to the proper course."[9] Like the compass on your dashboard, your "internal compass" is present even when you choose not to use it. But unlike the one in your car, you can't throw this compass away. Like it or not, it stays put. At some level, we all feel it. The internal compass produces a feeling that never leaves us. It keeps pointing to our true purpose.

Goethe said that people could not get rid of their true nature even if they threw it away. One's nature keeps coming back. Those on the right track will not feel pangs from the inner compass. Those who have moved away from their true nature, however, will feel a discomfort coming from within. More precisely, what they will feel is guilt for not becoming what they were meant to be.

I once had a client, whom I will call Judd, who demonstrated this discomfort in a most interesting way. At twenty-seven, Judd had earned a Ph.D. in sociology, had recently married, and was teaching at a community college. From a distance he looked fine. But Judd felt rumblings from within. Although he had earned everything he had accomplished, he felt guilt and discontent. He was an articulate man, but he could not put his situation into words.

At first, he could identify his problem only with the words, "Things aren't right." After a few sessions, he told me something that spoke to the heart of his turmoil. "I'll tell you something I haven't told anyone," he said.

"What's that?" I asked slowly.

"You know, . . . I don't have my own laugh."

"Tell me more," I begged quietly after a moment of silence.

"I don't," he said. "I really don't. I laugh like other people. I think it started in college, but it may have been before then. When I laugh, I can tell whose laugh I'm using. It's never mine. I think I lost mine sometime back. Sometimes I get scared that I've lost it forever."

Judd eventually found his own laughter, but not before a series of unusual events changed his life. This sociologist who had been studying people from his perch in higher education came to be touched by the plight of the homeless. As he became involved in this cause, Judd came alive. He began to contribute his time and the money he could afford. He didn't quit his job or leave his wife. He didn't have to turn his life upside down. By helping to feed the homeless, he fed his own soul. His well-nourished soul gave him a great laugh, a laugh that was sincere and honest. Judd found the missing piece. He was called to a cause that touched him deeply, and he gladly did what he could to meet the need.

Fortunately for Judd, he did not have far to go. Through his academic work he knew the statistics on the homeless. He knew all the theories. He had his opinions. He did not, however, know how the homeless sounded, felt, and smelled. He had seen the pictures but not the people. His step into the real was significant, but it was not as tumultuous as the moves others are called to make. He did not have to change orbits. He had only to take the next step.

Other people feel pulled to change their worlds. They feel the tug to take huge steps that could result in failure and abandonment. With such a pull, one might stand petrified in the face of possibilities, feeling too small or powerless to do what one believes one needs to do. This situation is much like the story of the woman who, while walking down the street, comes across a boy standing on the corner with a suitcase at his feet. When the woman asks him what he is doing, he reports that he is running away. When she asks him why he is waiting at the corner, he replies, "I'm not allowed to cross the street."

Sometimes we must cross the street. Maybe André Gide said it best: "One does not discover new lands without consenting to losing sight of the shore for a very long time."

The Essentials

Selecting a path is risky. Refusing to choose a direction, however, is certain self-destruction. We are called to move selected mountains. But which mountains are the right ones? How can you be sure in a world where there are so many mountains?

We have a difficult time distinguishing between an impulse

and a revelation. They can seem so similar, yet they are very different. No one should commit to an impulse. An impulse is a distraction rather than a destiny. It lures one away from a real calling.

We must settle this. We need to know the essential qualities that make a calling unique. They are these: service, thought, and feelings. Each in its turn is discussed below.

Service

Callings involve service to life. While some people are called to contribute to the welfare of their fellow human beings, others are pulled toward caring for animals or the environment. Service to one form of life is service to all.

Franz Schubert once claimed that he was "in the world only for the purpose of composing." He was, of course, wrong. Dead wrong. Completely wrong. Service to music is not enough. There invariably exists an element of service to life in all callings. Without this, one is led astray.

Schubert's mistake, unfortunately, is common among creative and artistic people. They get caught up in their gifts and turn away from their calling to serve others. This explains why many extraordinarily creative individuals have significant emotional and psychological problems. They confuse their talents with their mission in life. Your talents are only a portion of your calling. The largest part of your vision involves how you will use these gifts. It is never enough to compose or paint or write. These skills must be used in the service of a greater good.

Growing amounts of psychological research indicate that happiness is more likely to be found by those who dedicate themselves to causes larger than themselves. Service to life is the most human way to live. Service is a fundamental element in deciding whether or not you are being called in a particular direction. If there is not an element of service to life, or if there is no way that this road could lead to the service of life, then you are not being *called* to travel it. Impulses, confusion, fear, and selfishness may all, at times, feel like callings. We can begin to rule out false callings by simply asking: "What is this path's potential for service?"

If there exists the potential to serve, then there is the definite possibility that one is experiencing a genuine calling. Then one must perform the second litmus test — the examination by thought.

Thought

We can be called before we are ready. In other words, we may develop the awareness of a vision before we have the knowledge needed to reach that goal. We dream dreams; then we find out how to realize them. Callings can begin by hooking our curiosities. Sometimes the first sign of a calling occurs after we have seen something new and a voice inside whispers, "Isn't that interesting?" We are wise to pay close attention to this inner voice, but our missions always also involve our intellects. The voice of reason provides sound counsel. It helps us to understand what we are asked to do and helps us to complete our tasks successfully. A calling requires rational thought. It's not something that comes along and sweeps you mindlessly off your feet. You can plan, arrange, and prepare to answer it. You have to think it through. Before you commit, you must decide. Decisions need thought.

To accomplish your mission you need to focus your will, but you need not surrender it. No one else can force a calling upon you. You decide how you will move and which way you will go. You decide if and how you will approach your vision. This is an important point because it contradicts the notion that a calling is something you accept completely on faith, something you should comply with without consulting your intellect. Nothing could be further from the truth. When you are called, all of you is called. To fulfill a calling you will need your intelligence. A real calling can withstand scrutiny. It has no cause to deceive you. No calling asks you to accept it blindly. As you consider it you come to grasp it. Once your mind accepts your calling, you find you have a clearer focus on your goals.

As necessary and powerful as thought can be, however, there is at least one mystery your reason may never be able to solve: why you have been given your set of callings. You may never know the answer to "Why me?" but this is only a minor shortcoming — once people connect with their callings, the "why" is no longer important. The preoccupation with "Why me?" fades as they move into their missions. At this point they become much less self-centered.

As one thinks, one will be led. If one stays true to the learning trail, one comes to a place of passion and energy. This is the land of feelings.

Feelings

A friend of mine once, as a young man, went on an interview as part of the admission process to a prestigious medical school. He had worked hard to prepare for the meeting and developed what he believed to be appropriate responses to every possible question he might encounter. Well, the day of the interview came and he arrived at the university confident. Shortly into the interview, however, he ran into problems.

The interviewer asked him perhaps the most basic question of all, "Why do you want to be a physician?" My friend, of course, had this one memorized. He told his examiner that he wanted to be a doctor because he wanted to serve his fellow humans. He then pressed on with his response, trying to convince the man that serving humanity was his purpose in life. The interviewer sat and listened, carefully giving no indication as to the worthiness of my friend's response. Undaunted, my friend finished his short sermon and then leaned back in his chair, feeling secure that he had successfully answered this and was off to a solid start.

"I see," said the examiner, "that sounds marvelous. But there are many ways to serve humanity. If this is your sole motive — and a noble motive it is — you could follow any one of countless career paths. So let me ask you again, Why do you want to be a physician?" My friend hadn't prepared for this one. He tried to recover, but he couldn't. He didn't receive an invitation to enter that particular institution. It was the cost of wisdom: on that day he learned that thinking about a calling is not enough; one must have a feeling, a passion, for it.

The world has many needs with endless opportunities to serve. Of these, the mind selects what might be interesting, intriguing. As curiosity pulls one in a certain direction, the stage becomes set for another essential ingredient in a calling — the feeling. A healthy person has a vibrant curiosity. Curiosity is a life force. It leads us to places where we need to be. Among the things that attract our curiosities, there emerge a few that give rise to our passion. If we allow ourselves to think, we will know the curiosity. If we allow ourselves to feel, we will become passionate.

When passion and curiosity unite we become, as they say, "carried away." It's as if something much larger than ourselves is moving us in a direction we love. We may feel fear of what lies ahead. We may feel anger if our cause takes us places where life has been violated. Here we learn that healthy anger can fuel passion.

There are two more important points that need to be made here. First, being carried away, in its healthy form, still requires and involves a person's will. We _decide_ that this is the way we want to go; we agree, after thoughtful consideration, that this particular course is the correct one. We can also be carried away in an unhealthy manner. In this case, a person acts on pure impulse. Major life decisions are made on a whim, in ignorance. An example might help here. One night I had a dream that I was a milkman. It felt great—there were happy, uncomplicated, beautiful sunny mornings, and everyone was smiling. The dream reminded me that when I was small I wanted very much to be a milkman. The next morning when I awoke I asked myself with a smile if I should quit everything and search for a life as a milkman. But the invitation didn't stand the examination of a rational mind. It was a pleasant dream. I hope it comes again. But it was not a calling. There are other things I need to do. The voyages that are chosen by our hearts and minds can be healthy, productive, and, in some cases, may last a lifetime. The mindless excursions, however, usually end in disappointment.

The second point is this: sometimes we are unaware of how much we love what we are doing. Even when we are on exactly the right track, our lives may seem less than passionate. Take, for example, the mother who feels taken for granted and less than enthralled spending her days tending to the needs of little ones. She may have lost the "carried away" feeling and may even have begun to wonder if she is where she is supposed to be. Then comes the day when her first-grader doesn't come home from school on time. After a few more minutes pass, she begins to feel fear and becomes a bit disoriented. More time goes by, and the feeling intensifies. Then, as if out of nowhere, the child walks through the door to her mother's frantic hug. It is an instant of passion in which this mother is reminded that she is on her proper course.

Of the three dimensions of a calling, service and thought

provide direction. Feeling provides the energy and the determination to get there. Feeling also supplies the passion to stay the proper course. It's the fuel, the fire, the love.

The feeling part is the hardest to put into words, but this is as it should be. If we had words for all the nuances of emotion, then we would be more likely to intellectualize and analyze feelings to the point where they would lose their enchantment and energy. It's best that feelings can't be completely described. If they could, they would no longer be feelings. They would be thoughts. There is indeed an element of mystery in feelings. Yet, ironically, without feelings we could never feel certainty.

When our desire to serve, our thought, and our feelings all come together, we find ourselves doing what's right. You will not find yourself in your right place until you integrate these three elements.

In their book *Some Do Care,* Anne Colby and William Damon describe, in depth, the lives of twenty-three extraordinarily altruistic people.[10] These individuals have lived lives of accomplishment and great moral courage. Among their interesting conclusions, Colby and Damon found that "the sense of compulsion simply to do the right thing runs throughout" the lives of these people. People who have found their mission seem to dedicate themselves to doing what's right. As Martin Luther King Jr. said: "My obligation is to do the right thing. The rest is in God's hands."

Colby and Damon observe that for the people in their research, "the right path seems so clearly defined that it rules out all alternatives."[11] People with a mission are those who allow themselves to see their path.

The Rewards

The Scottish historian and philosopher Thomas Carlyle once wrote, "Blessed is he who has found his work; let him ask no other blessedness." Maybe Carlyle was a workaholic. Perhaps this statement is a bit extreme, but it moves us close to what may be a crucial truth. If we enlarge Carlyle's picture a bit, we find something important.

Fortunate indeed is the soul who has found his or her own true nature and calling; that person should little reason to ask for much more. But self-discovery is a lifelong process. Our true nature changes as do our callings. Your mission at age ten may differ from your course at age thirty. Still, at each point that your path becomes new to you, there is a revelation, a celebration, and then a courageous serenity. Confusion decreases. Frustration lifts. Life is good, even if the work is hard.

All the stories you read as a child about discovering treasures, magical genies, and lands of enchantment pale when compared with the marvelous experience of finding you. Confidence builds and self-consciousness disappears as you encounter the _This Is Me_ Experience (TIME). This seems to be what people mean when they say, "My _time_ has come." This is the moment when you find your right track. With it comes energy — sometimes a tidal wave of energy. When you become aware of your purpose, you feel useful and needed. When useful and needed are added together, they produce the wonderful feeling of belonging. Living your calling may cost you millions of dollars, and it may even shorten your life. But it takes you to places where money and years may not concern you.

"One should not search for an abstract meaning of life," wrote Viktor Frankl. "Everyone has his own specific vocation or mission in life to carry out a concrete assignment that demands fulfillment. Therein he cannot be replaced, nor can his life be repeated. Thus, everyone's task is as unique as is his specific opportunity to implement it."[12] You cannot be replaced. Nor can your life be repeated. You have your gifts, and this is your time.

Your task may be difficult. You may be called to move a mountain or to build a new one. And when you are through, if you ever are, there may be no applause, no accolades, only the knowledge that you moved in your true direction and did what only you could have done.

Dag Hammarskjöld spoke wisely when he said, "Cry. Cry if you must. But do not complain. The path has chosen you. And in the end you will say 'thank you.'" One of the most interesting facts of life is that we become grateful to those we have served. We come to appreciate the opportunities we have had to serve, as arduous as they may have been at the time. Not only can we survive the hardships; we can survive gratefully.

The path that chooses us brings to us our purpose in life. It explains, in its own way, why we are alive. And, as Nietzsche made clear, "He who has a why to live can bear with almost any how."

The human spirit aches for direction. Once we discover what we are to accomplish, the ache turns into focused energy. Then we can survive all that we need to survive. Our only real enemy is distraction. Yet as we live our callings, our own power grows. We feel more in control of our lives, less vulnerable to distraction. Envy, for example (one of the most distracting distractions), melts away as we touch the feeling that we have found our purpose in life. Our destiny is not sculpted by the social world. Envy has no place in the soul of someone who is living his or her call.

Personal power, self-acceptance, energy, direction, and contentment come with a calling. So do hard work and sacrifice. If Nietzsche was right, then a goal in life will carry us through the tough times. And if Hammarskjöld is correct, then ultimately we will feel gratitude for our callings, no matter how much pain they may have brought us.

Believing in and responding to a call may involve what some might call faith. A calling doesn't present itself to the five senses. When a calling is felt, however, one gets a glimpse of the rewards. It's that momentary look at all that is possible, all that your life can be. It may not last long enough to describe. But it leaves a special feeling.

I don't think that a calling's primary purpose is to reward the one who is called. Still, there are rewards for those who live their callings.

At the Beginning

One does not actually choose an entire path. One can only choose a beginning to a path. That's really all we see: the beginning.

We can imagine and hope, just as a young couple imagines the future of their child in the minutes after learning of the pregnancy. An artist can imagine a completed work before she or he has bought paints. I'm sure many biology majors see themselves curing cancer. The dreams can feel so real, we almost feel we can touch them. We like the feeling of having control of what lies ahead.

We do not, however, control our callings. We can hope and dream, but we should never become rigid dreamers. We must give our aspirations the freedom to grow and to grow old. A man at thirty may dream of career success. At forty his hopes may form around his children. At fifty his church and community may occupy his visions. Upon turning sixty he may realize, perhaps for the first time, that he loves life and always has. At seventy he may dedicate his life to expressing gratitude.

The initial callings give way to larger callings. We don't control this. Perhaps the most common reason people refuse to accept the existence of callings is that callings keep them from achieving complete control of their lives. We don't invent our callings. They come to us. We don't determine their timing, power, or form. They can, for instance, be difficult to understand and thereby remove the certainty that made life cozy. When we come to understand our callings, explaining them to others can be frustrating. In the process of answering our callings, we can feel more than a little confused and appear more than a little lost.

Some time ago I met an attorney, a friend of a friend. I knew part of his story before we even spoke. He had been a very successful corporate lawyer who earned large amounts of money and prestige. Then, for no obvious reason, he quit. Few saw it coming. Fewer still explained it well. He just quit. Then came a bigger surprise. He took a job working with poor people, mostly folks who were involved in housing disputes. His salary dropped to a small fraction of what it had been.

When I met this man I knew it might be the only chance I would ever have to speak to him. So I asked him flat out, "Why did you do it?" I worried that he might resent the question, coming as it did from a virtual stranger, but he didn't appear to. It became obvious, however, that he couldn't articulate an answer. "I needed to," he replied at last in a soft, thoughtful tone. My first impulse was to ask for more detail. But a voice inside told me to leave the man alone, that he had already told me all I needed to know. It was obvious that it was all that he had needed to know. I knew that this man was entitled to some confusion. He had moved courageously to the place where he needed to be. His move made others question his sanity. Besides this, he had no way of knowing what he was in for. Still, he moved.

In the beginning we see only the first few steps. We can imagine and hope for much more, but it takes courage to move without promises and guarantees. It takes daring to move beyond the first steps, but the courage invested in the beginning pays great dividends down the line. The shaky, newborn spirit grows stronger. The path may not become easier, but the person walking it becomes more courageous. It has been said that the journey of a thousand miles begins with a single step. Once people find the courage to take that step, they are changed forever — changed because they now know how to find courage. Courage is easier to acquire once one knows where to find it. Different people find it in different places. Some find their courage within themselves. Others reach far beyond themselves to grasp the strength they need. Although all courage may ultimately come from the same source, people meet it in different places.

Courage, of course, does not remove fear. Rather, it provides us with the spirit necessary to walk through fear. Since we are never called unless we are also empowered, each calling comes equipped with enough courage to answer it. There will still be fear, sometimes a great deal. In an earlier work, _Facing Fear,_ I suggested that perhaps courage and callings come from the same place.[13] If this is true, then you may find your courage in the place where you hear your calling. And you might hear your calling in the place where you find your courage.

Whatever your situation happens to be, the first step can be the biggest. No matter how many inspirational books you read or motivational lectures you hear, making a commitment may be fraught with some anxiety. How many great minds have made a point of encouraging others to conquer their fear of the first step! Goethe, for instance, wrote that "until one is committed, there is hesitancy, the chance to draw back, always ineffectiveness. Concerning all acts of initiative or creation there is one elementary truth, the ignorance of which kills countless ideas and splendid plans: *that the moment one definitely commits oneself, then Providence moves too.*"

This is the stuff graduation speeches are made of: heroes and sages at microphones imploring their audiences to seize their opportunities, beseeching their listeners to contribute as only they can. It's not coincidence that those we identify as moral exemplars tend to present and repeat a similar theme. These are usually people who took the risks necessary to maximize their personal power and fulfill their lives. Then, when asked to guide others, they pound home a message that insists people take that first step in the direction they believe is right.

After that first step is taken — if it is taken boldly — courage and energy grow. "Anyone writing a creative work knows that you open, you yield yourself, and the book talks to you and builds itself," remarked Joseph Campbell.[14] Eventually you may learn that the path has chosen you. And you will be grateful.

Conclusion

Callings pull us to think, feel, and serve. Those courageous enough to answer their callings reap a variety of rewards. While we can describe some of these benefits specifically, it seems more helpful here to say simply that the process by which they are rewarded has some similarity with the way that a seed is rewarded by growing toward the sun. It's as if the seed were called by the sun. This seed becomes what it is to become. In the process it finds its own true nature.

The path you are called to may be the most difficult you could imagine. Still, it is the right one. The right path never goes away, even if you leave it for a time. It waits for you. You don't own this road. You can't force it to move as you would like. At the same time, the road cannot control you. You can leave it or choose never to travel it.

Some seeds never grow. Some seeds grow magnificently.

A Well-Known Secret

Every calling is great when greatly pursued.
— OLIVER WENDELL HOLMES

There are at least two ways to learn something: you can experience it yourself and/or learn about it from someone you respect. This chapter concerns the latter and has much ground to cover, for many thoroughly esteemed leaders and scholars have expressed a firm belief in their callings. In certain cases you have to read the fine print to find it, but it's there nonetheless.

A calling may indeed be a spiritual phenomenon — one that originates in and ultimately leads to a spiritual world. But callings have also been the fascination of many who might not be categorized as clergy, mystic, saint, or theologian. Callings have been addressed by historians, scientists, and philosophers and have captured the interest of physicians, politicians, artists, and writers.

Callings come to everyone, not just the royalty and religious. One of the most common misconceptions about callings is that a person must be "spiritual" in order to hear one. This is erroneous, way off, a big mistake. The truth is that callings have *brought* many people to a spiritual life. People who would never have listened to clergy, mystics, saints, or theologians have, through their own experiences, come to believe in callings.

Sometimes we find it hard to believe something until we hear about it from someone whose ideas we value. In the end, of course, the most important convictions are our own. So that our convictions may be educated convictions, let us examine the evidence of callings that comes from the secular sector. Perhaps leaving theology and connotations of religious vocations aside can lead us to what might be considered a more objective point of view.

We can begin with the ancient Greeks. Socrates claimed to have heard voices "murmuring in my ears, like the sound of the flute in the ears of the mystics."[1] Unfortunately for Socrates, it was this kind of talk that eventually led to his execution. Consequently, his students and followers began to downplay divine inspiration and developed more rational (i.e., less spiritual) philosophies instead.[2] This change of thinking has continued its impact into the present day.

But the execution of Socrates did not completely kill the belief that knowledge could be received from the spiritual world. Plato, for instance, in his dialogue _Ion,_ asserted that poets received their work like a bolt from the blue and were "possessed by a spirit not their own."[3] The notion of a calling may have been wounded, but it never died.

Twentieth-century philosopher and psychologist William James advised that we "steer safely between the opposite dangers of believing too little or of believing too much." While most of us today make great efforts to protect ourselves from the danger of believing too much, I'm afraid we've made ourselves the victims of believing too little. Our civilization tends to give almost total credence to the five senses, tending to deny the existence of things that cannot be validated by one or more of these five. We have become our own executioners, persecuting ourselves if we dare to consider that there is more to the universe than what we can see, smell, taste, hear, and feel.

I suppose there are many ways to lift this self-oppression. One strategy is to find someone to lead you away from it — someone who inspires you to make your own interpretations, someone who gives you permission and incentive to reach your own conclusions. Good leaders help people find their callings. Indeed, effective leaders are those who follow their own callings. In *Managing as a Performing Art*, Peter Vail says, "All true leadership is indeed spiritual leadership. ...Leadership is concerned about bringing out the best in people. As such, one's best is tied intimately to one's spirit." And James Autry, president of Meredith Corporation's magazine group, contends that "good management is largely a matter of love,...a calling,...a sacred trust."[4]

A good leader can be the best example of how a calling is lived. The leader is someone who moves with courage and determination even when the rewards for doing so seem nonexistent, a person whose motives are not prestige or material gain but rather a loyalty to a value and a mission. We might ask: Who/What leads a good leader? The answer, I think, is clear: good leaders follow their visions. In his Pulitzer Prize–winning book *Leadership*, James MacGregor Burnes speaks of the *vocation* of leadership. Specifically, he describes President Woodrow Wilson as having been "devoted to the vocation of leadership as an elevating force."[5] Good leadership has a way of lifting followers to new heights. This may manifest itself in greater self-confidence or the development of the leadership skills of the followers. Good leaders help their followers move away from fear and distractions. Good leaders help people mature to the point where they no longer need other people to lead them.

Perhaps there is even more on the legacy of a good leader. Could the exposure to a good leader actually help someone find his or her own calling? While being subject to a tyrant could be crippling, could not an encounter with a good leader be empowering enough to aid one in finding one's own way? In the search for our callings, wouldn't we be well served by experiencing others who have found theirs?

There are many, many fascinating questions about the nature of callings. There are also numerous ways to go about answering these. Even science, with its sea of skeptics, has contributed to our understanding of this mysterious phenomenon.

Science

Someone once remarked that, unlike universities, knowledge is not divided into departments. In other words, the study of literature is an essential part of the study of human behavior. Sociology, economics, and history are each seriously limited fields without the information the others have to offer. And science without an examination of spirituality will inevitably lead to frustration and disappointment.

For decades the field of psychology fought to make itself a science. Science had precision, tangible results, and perhaps, most importantly, respect. As a "hard" science it would take its place alongside such venerable disciplines as physics, biology, and chemistry. These fields of white coats and breakthrough discoveries had established themselves firmly in the hallowed halls of academia as well as in the American culture. It wasn't long, however, before the boat began to rock. Early in the twentieth century, scholars emerged who taught ideas that could not be refuted or validated through scientific methodology. Psychology, which had so wanted to be a science, began to understand that it had much to learn from the folks in the theology department.

Carl Jung was one of the first voices heard. Once a disciple of Sigmund Freud, Jung went on to separate himself from Freud and become one of the most important and courageous thinkers of our time. This separation is itself significant because in the process of growing into independence, Jung came to know himself as a "called personality." It was at this point in his life that he stopped thinking of himself as a young man choosing a path in life and, instead, came to believe that there was a particular path calling him. This calling affected him deeply. Twenty years after hearing his own calling he wrote:

> True personality always has vocation, which acts like the law of God from which there is no escape. Who has vocation hears the voice of the inner man; he is *called*. Now vocation is not the prerogative of great personalities, but also belongs to the small ones. But it happens to not a few to be summoned by the individual voice, whereupon they are at once differentiated from the others and feel themselves confronted by a problem that the others do not know about.[6]

That problem that others do not know about is what we are called to solve. It is our challenge, and it can be discovered only if we are willing to *emerge* as an independent, courageous being. While other psychotherapists were focusing on eliminating problems, Jung treated people by helping them find the problems (i.e., challenges) that were meant specifically for them. The belief that people need to emerge into their true selves became the essence of Jung's brand of psychotherapy. He encouraged his patients to pursue their own way, to discover the challenges that were meant only for them. Psychotherapy was to Jung a process of self-discovery, a process of finding one's calling.

His experiences with patients working to find their true selves led him to a fascinating conclusion:

> Among all my patients in the second half of life — that is to say over thirty-five — there has not been one whose problem in the last resort was not that of finding a religious outlook on life. It is safe to say that every one of them fell ill because he had lost that which the living religions of every age have given their followers, and none of them has really healed who did not regain his religious outlook.[7]

To Jung, a "religious outlook" meant an understanding of where one belongs in life and what one's purpose is. A religious outlook becomes such a natural part of some people's beings that they may not (consciously) realize that it's there. But if it gets lost, the void, the missing piece, can feel enormous. Although the pain can be medicated to some extent, as Jung pointed out, there can be no real healing until the religious outlook is regained. Carl Jung emerged with a cause. Trained as a scientist, he took what he had learned and moved beyond the restrictions of a single discipline. At that point he became a true scholar and humanitarian.

There were others who took science to a spiritual level. William James boldly asserted that we could not possibly understand the human condition without exploring the nature of religious experience. Trained as a physician, James grew into a philosopher and then followed his curiosity into the study of psychology. So important were his contributions that, to this day, he is widely considered the father of American psychology. James was a man who could transcend boundaries. He moved courageously toward answers. He knew the value and the limitations of science.

On the subject of callings, James once wrote, "There are moments of sentimental and mystical experience that carry an enormous sense of inner authority and illumination with them when they come."[8] These moments can lead to lasting changes in personality such as "a new zest which adds itself like a gift to life, and takes the form of either lyrical enchantment or of appeal to earnestness and heroism." The changes could also include "an assurance of safety and a temper of peace, and, in relation to others, a preponderance of loving affections."[9] In the end, the "inner voice" could lead one to the "ecstasy of happiness."

We are left to decide for ourselves the nature of the inner authority. Jung and James both suggested that we consider the possibility that our inner source of wisdom may be the voice of God. But they were both tolerant of the need in people to consider a variety of possibilities. They knew that finding one's inner authority can take a good deal of effort. Those who already believe in God may ask, "What else could it be? What else is there to consider? What other force could possibly guide human beings in our efforts to find where we really belong? What other force could lead to the illumination that James described?"

But of course many alternative explanations have been offered. Freud, for instance, claimed that we are driven by biological instincts. They are present at birth and remain with us throughout life. They are our core. We are driven by a biological essence. Then came the behaviorists, who believed that behavior is shaped by rewards and punishments. You become the things you are reinforced to become — be you saint or sinner, shy or outgoing, or something in-between. This theory suggests that we are not guided from within but by conditions that exist in our environment.

The behaviorists felt confident that they had finally made a science of the study of human conduct. One example of this confidence was a statement made by one of behaviorism's founding fathers, J. B. Watson. "Give me a dozen healthy infants, well-formed, and my own specified world to bring them up in," wrote Watson in 1924, "and I'll guarantee to take any one of them at random and train him to become any type of specialist I might select — doctor, lawyer, artist, merchant-chief and, yes, even beggar-man and thief."[10] The imagined power was intoxicating. Watson was talking about the utopia that had eluded humankind since the beginning of time. Finally, we had the technology to "build" it. Like every other utopian design, however, this one failed. Neither Watson nor anyone else could make good on his claim. Now, over half a century later, his statement is remembered as little more than hubris and fantasy.

The behaviorists never have addressed the spiritual dimension of human nature. It is, they say, unobservable, unmeasurable, unscientific. They have been determined to remain within the boundaries of science. So it was during the early and middle part of the twentieth century. People were told by the majority of their experts that spirituality played no part in the formula that determined their behavior or mental health. Time, however, produced more and more critics of this prevailing view. Instincts and reinforcers could not explain the experience of the awakening or revelation that enters people's lives. Nor could they adequately explain sacrifice. People routinely surrender self-serving rewards for the sake of a more moral alternative. This wouldn't seem possible for a race of people who only acted for self-gratification.

No, more was needed. While respecting the contribution of Freud and the behaviorists, social scientists in the early 1960s began to understand that the theories could not explain the full range of human behavior. Specifically (and this relates directly to our purposes), they began to see that we needed a greater knowledge of what James called the inner authority and what Jung referred to as the guiding powers of the unconscious.

Things took an interesting turn with the rise of the human potential movement. Among this group's central tenets stood the belief that everyone is born with a certain potential. This potential needs to be fulfilled or "actualized." People are believed to be pulled in their own directions. These paths are built on the gifts and talents that we come into the world with. As author and psychologist Rollo May wrote, "Every organism has one and only one central need in life, to fulfill its own potentialities."[11]

The idea that everyone is born with a mission gained support with the popular writings of Viennese psychiatrist Viktor Frankl. Frankl, a former inmate in the concentration camps during the Holocaust, developed the theory that human beings have one pervasive drive in life — to find meaning. Unlike other existential thinkers who claimed that people create or imagine meaning in what is essentially a meaningless existence, Frankl insisted that each human life has a unique purpose. Our task is not to create meaning but to *find* it. Mental health and happiness come to us as a result of finding the meaning of our lives.

During this era, psychology became fascinated with the nature of human potential. How far can people grow? If someone were completely psychologically and emotionally healthy, what would that person be like? Instead of focusing on mental illness as Freud and others had, this new group of researchers began to study the world of mental health.

This new group found its hero in one of the most important psychologists of our time, Abraham Maslow. Maslow, a master researcher and one-time president of the American Psychological Association, dedicated his professional life to developing a psychology of healthy human functioning. He called this upper level of human functioning "self-actualization." While this concept is difficult to explain, Maslow summarized self-actualization this way:

> For the purpose of this discussion, it may be loosely described as the full use and exploitation of talents, capacities, potentialities, etc. Such people seem to be fulfilling themselves and to be doing the best that they are capable of doing, reminding us of Nietzsche's exhortation, "Become what thou art!" They are people who have developed or are developing to the full stature of which they are capable.[12]

Self-actualized people look for meaning and purpose and are not content with a life that is only safe and secure. They look for their tasks. They refuse to remove themselves from adversity if that is where they belong. According to Maslow, self-actualized individuals

> are in general strongly focused on problems outside themselves. In current terminology they are problem centered rather than ego centered. They generally are not problems for themselves and are generally not much concerned about themselves; e.g., as contrasted with the ordinary introspectiveness that one finds in insecure people. _These individuals customarily have some mission in life, some problem outside themselves which enlists much of their energies._[13]

Maslow insisted that "what a man _can_ be he _must_ be. He must be true to his own nature." In this sense we are called to be what we are. We are called to fulfill our potential. In fact, Maslow's biographer, Edward Hoffman, wrote that self-actualization involves a "calling" to service from the external, day-to-day world, not only a yearning from within.[14]

Maslow's theory suggests that we enter this world with a potential; we enter this world with a calling.

One of the most intriguing, yet unresolved, aspects of Maslow's theory concerns the source of our callings. Although Maslow was a staunch atheist, many of his writings appear to be written by someone about to abandon his atheism. Unfortunately, Maslow died suddenly of a heart attack at the age of sixty-two. Whether or not his atheism would have given way to faith will never be known. We are left to wonder how he might have explained why certain people have particular talents. He believed we have a psychological obligation to be true to ourselves, but he never considered that we might have a moral obligation as well.

We must find for ourselves the source of our callings. We must answer for ourselves who or what selected us for our missions in life. This, Maslow noted, is one of the core features of self-actualizers. He once remarked that "fulfillment in life never comes from following the crowd, but only from being faithful to one's yearnings and talents."[15]

Although Maslow did not clearly identify the source of our callings, he did describe experiences that might lead us to our source. He called these peak-experiences. During the course of his life he defined peak-experiences in different ways, and as he aged, his descriptions became more and more detailed. The term "peak-experience," he wrote, "is a generalization for the best moments of the human being, for the happiest moments of life, for experiences of ecstasy, rapture, bliss of the greatest joy."[16] A peak-experience is

> an episode, or a spurt in which the powers of the person come together in a particularly efficient and enjoyable way, and in which he is more integrated and less split, more open for experience, more perfectly expressive or spontaneous, or fully functioning, more creative, more

humorous, more ego-transcending, etc. He becomes in these episodes more truly himself, more perfectly actualizing his potentialities, close to the core of his Being, more fully human.[17]

Maslow observed that the impact of peak-experiences could be so great that they could give meaning to life itself. They were, in at least certain cases, enough to prove that life is worthwhile. Moreover, they could put people in touch with their callings. These spontaneous seizures of wonder, awe, reverence, humility, and surrender can connect one with one's purpose for living. Interestingly, at times Maslow — the atheist — used theological concepts to elaborate on the nature of these experiences. For instance, in his book _Religions, Values, and Peak-Experiences,_ he wrote, "I have likened the peak-experience in a metaphor to a visit to a personally defined heaven in which the person then returns to earth." After this "visit" the person tends to become "more loving and more accepting, and so he becomes more spontaneous and honest and innocent." Later in the same work Maslow made the point that a "single glimpse of heaven is enough to confirm its existence even if it's never experienced again."[18]

It bears repeating that Maslow was a respected researcher and a leader in his field. He was by no means a minor player trifling on the lunatic fringe. Nor was he the first to investigate what he called peak-experiences. In 1962 English researcher Margaritha Laski published an empirical study that independently confirmed much of Maslow's work. In her book _Ecstasy,_[19] she examined people's ecstatic experiences in everyday life, such as watching a beautiful sunrise or walking along the shore. Laski's research supported the power of the ecstatic (or peak-) experience.

Maslow believed that in a peak-experience the doors open, if only momentarily, and people get a precious opportunity to see a greater meaning. It's an event that lifts one higher, makes one wiser. The peak-experience is a key to unrealized potential. It can also be the point where someone is introduced to a calling.

The consequences of such experiences vary. Although people respond uniquely, the effects of these episodes are thought to be always healthy. I'm not aware of any evidence that points to a negative consequence of a peak-experience. Most of Maslow's work described how the experience makes healthy people healthier. But health is not a prerequisite, for he also mentioned the healing power of peak-experiences. He wrote, briefly, how these events have taken people with emotional and psychological problems and moved them closer to self-actualization.

In one lecture on the characteristics of peak-experiences he explained that "a peak-experience is a complete, though momentary, loss of fear, anxiety, inhibition, defense and control."[20] Thus it seems that the peak-experience may be a mechanism through which a person loses a fear of life. We might consider it a corrective action that moves us closer to where we should be.

In *Religion, Values, and Peak-Experiences,* Maslow again touches on the healing power of these events: "In my own experience I have two subjects who, because of such an experience, were totally, immediately, and permanently cured of (in one case) chronic anxiety neurosis and (in the other case) of strong obsessional thoughts of suicide."[21] At this point a person more religious than Maslow might have suggested that what he was labeling peak-experiences might actually be miracles. It's disappointing that he did not give more time and attention to the healing qualities of these special episodes. As it is, we are left to ponder what really cured these two individuals.

One can't help but wonder if the two subjects ultimately

became more spiritual in the process of their recovery. Carl Jung indicated that his patients were looking for a "religious outlook on life" and that none could be truly cured until they gained a spiritual orientation. Can a peak-experience help someone find or regain a spiritual orientation? Maslow leaves the question unanswered, but the notion that spiritual experiences can alleviate what appear to be psychological maladies has gained support since his death. An atheist who insisted that there is more to the human condition than instincts and conditioning, Maslow took science about as far as it can go. He then asserted that we are capable of going further. If he had lived longer, he may have become a scientist-theologian.

Today much of mental health care includes a spiritual dimension. Psychiatric facilities now usually include pastoral care in their treatment programs. Also, the spiritually based Twelve Step program that serves as the foundation for Alcoholics Anonymous (as well as most other "anonymous" groups) further attests to the growing recognition that spiritual awakenings are capable of healing psychological disorders from anxiety to addiction.

Paul R. Fleischman, psychiatrist and former faculty member at the Yale University School of Medicine, points to the spiritual and psychological need to answer one's calling:

> Patients will talk about their need to find their tasks, their jobs, their work to be done. The need to feel useful, used, relevant, connected, a spoke on the wheel, a voice in the chorus is the need for a calling. This need is the bedrock of human life. A calling provides a foundation for all human activity, and particularly for utilizing one's personal facets or individuating characteristics.[22]

In other words, your calling joins you with the rest of humanity while it draws you out and encourages you to emerge as a singular character. It asks for union and individuality, each acting in harmony with the other. It asks that we each make our special contributions to enhance the health, well-being, and beauty of the universe. With a calling comes both an identity and a purpose.

How we receive our callings (which will be covered in more detail in chapters 4 and 5) is not a simple issue. There is more to receiving a calling than peak-experiences. While many have claimed to have found meaning through those episodes, most people find their missions in a more gradual way. To these folks, a calling doesn't come like a bolt of lightning. It's more of a learning experience, a wisdom that ripens over the seasons. Further, many of the people who are most skeptical about the existence of callings are those who have acquired their paths so gracefully that they are unaware of any special force trying to guide them. These souls might explain how they found their way by merely saying, "It's just natural."

The old bolt-of-lightning experience can make a believer out of even the most sincere doubter. But not everyone needs to be struck by lightning in order to accept that lightning exists. Even if you acquired your electricity in doses so small that you didn't feel your power grow, you may want to stop and consider the source. Personal power increases tremendously when you understand that your mission, no matter how it was received, was meant exclusively for you. It's your job to do, and it could not possibly be done by anyone else but you. Find the source of your power and you will never be without energy.

Callings, as I have said, come in many ways. Maslow described the wonderful moments that bring new wisdom and a clearer sense of meaning. At the other end of the continuum we find other, more painful experiences that bring us an equally clear message. Tragedy can turn our lives upside-down and pull us back and forth before, finally, setting us at the beginning of a brand new path. Mental health professionals have long observed this phenomenon. Harvard psychiatrist Robert Lifton named it "the survivor mission." People struck by tragedy often take that awful experience and use it to find their life's work. The examples are countless. It's as if these people's mission comes to them in a single sentence: "Something needs to be done about this!"

Victims of child abuse go on to establish support groups for other survivors. Cancer patients and their loved ones often find themselves deeply involved in fund raising for cancer research. Drives to make communities safer are frequently led by those who have been touched directly by the violence. And those who have seen the horrors of war are sometimes our most articulate and driven spokespeople for peace.

Psychologist Al Siebert has studied this phenomenon for over thirty years. He claims that people with survivor personalities are those who

- have survived a major crisis,

- have surmounted the crisis through personal effort,

- have emerged from the experience with previously unknown strengths and abilities, and

- have in retrospect found value in the experience.[23]

The survivor mission is a call for heroes. Of course, people in these circumstances rarely think of themselves as heroes. They are focused on their missions; they are not inclined to laud themselves. It wasn't until I understood this that I could begin to understand what anthropologist Ernest Becker meant when he said that "our central calling, our main task on this planet, is the heroic."[24] Sometimes it takes overwhelming pain and suffering to help us find our way.

Heroes emerge as people scream from deep inside, "Enough is enough!"

Becker, a Pulitzer Prize–winning author, believed that it is difficult for most people to hear their central calling because they are not raised to be heroes. We have this inner need that is not given encouragement, or even permission, to voice itself. Small children show real potential to be heroes. But as this urge is ignored, the potential withers. When it dies, so does part of the person. Becker, incidentally, was not the first or only sage to preach the human need for heroism. William James, for example, wrote that "mankind's common instinct for reality...has always held the world to be essentially a theatre for heroism." The same sentiment can also be found in the thoughts of the great philosophers Emerson and Nietzsche.[25]

Whether or not adversity is essential to heroism, I don't know. It does appear, however, that they often coexist. Further, because we are unique individuals, we each must become a hero in our own way. No two heroes are alike. As with all callings, this one brings out the specialness in individuals. Becker described this beautifully when he suggested that "if you are going to be a hero then you must give a gift." This gift must be *your* gift. You must provide something in a way that only you can.

So what can we conclude at this point? We have heard evidence that callings can be found during our most wonderful and ecstatic moments. We have also heard support for the hypothesis that callings can be realized as a result of our most devastating personal trials. But we are not yet prepared to say (scientifically) if these experiences *produce* callings or if they create the conditions in which we are more likely to hear our callings. In other words, as scientists, we still cannot identify the source from which callings originate.

Our investigation, though, is by no means over. What

about those times between the highs and the lows when life seems to be moving you in a particular direction? These are the times when mistakes, accidents, and coincidences seem to be pointing you somewhere. The easiest explanation is that you're just being paranoid or delusionary, but then there is that little voice deep inside that insists on advising you: "Maybe there is more to it." How these kinds of experiences affect human behavior hasn't received much theoretical speculation, never mind scientific study. But what little there is remains pertinent to our interest in callings.

In 1982 Stanford University psychologist Albert Bandura published an article in the prestigious journal *American Psychologist* entitled "The Psychology of Chance Encounters and Life Paths."[26] The central thesis of this essay is that chance encounters play a prominent role in shaping the course of human lives. These encounters seem to come out of nowhere, for no reason. Yet they can have a profound impact on what we become. Bandura uses as an example a hypothetical situation of a college student who enrolls in a particular class for no other reason than because the computer put him there or because that class was the only one offered at the desired time. The student then encounters a truly inspiring teacher who has a decisive influence on his choice of career.

Maybe a more common example would be marriage. It seems that so many marriages begin by accident. Two people who should have been somewhere else stumble across each other in the strangest way. And then they end up spending their lives together. "Chance encounters affect life paths," wrote Bandura, and it is interesting how often events that seemed accidental at the time become, in hindsight, much more than merely haphazard. All those lifetime partnerships that began by "luck" and all those marvelous opportunities that just happened to arise become in retrospect less and less accidental.

Louis Pasteur noted that accidental discoveries come to those who have prepared for them. "Chance favors the prepared mind," he advised. In other words, accidental discoveries are not all that accidental. They tend to come to those who work, often very hard, in the arena where the discovery is made. Pasteur's observation makes the point that doors are more likely to open for people who walk toward them. Explorers are more likely to make the big discovery. It's unlikely that nonexplorers will stumble on to much of anything.

Doors open for people who are open to this kind of revelatory experience, for those who are open to surprise and willing to learn from what life offers. We could paraphrase Pasteur's remark and suggest that chance favors the open mind. Or, perhaps more accurately, chance favors the open spirit. The open spirit seizes the message. And the greatest regret we can ever know is the tragedy of not passing through the special doors that opened just for us.

At times these accidental events don't create anything new as much as they lead to a greater appreciation of the old. Helen Haste, a British developmental psychologist who has written about moral development, holds that many morally dedicated people are affected by "triggering events." These are sudden, unexpected occurrences that create powerful emotional responses that "trigger" a reexamination of one's life choices.[27]

Maybe it's the time your car spins around on an icy highway. In that instant before you regain control, something grabs you. As your car settles, you feel moved. Maybe you've skidded on frozen roads before, but this time it's different. This time the experience leaves you with a mandate to review your priorities and perhaps create new ones. Or maybe it's the homeless person who surprises you by asking you for money. Again, even though this may not be new to you, this time it's different. Maybe this particular person catches your attention because he looks like someone you once knew. Whatever the reason, you start looking at all the homeless in a new light. A momentary exchange with a needy stranger can lead to a small awakening that may, ultimately, lead to a grand awakening.

Timing seems to have a lot to do with this. What you don't notice on one day may jolt you, even transform you, on another. Is this accidental? Is it without purpose or design? Or is there more to it?

Well, here again we have reached a point where science can take us no further. Science can't be sure why these apparently accidental events occur. Even if it concedes that chance encounters are part of a calling, we are still left with the question of where the calling begins.

We have considered peak-experiences, tragedy, and chance encounters. All have led to some similar conclusions and at least one crucial question. All three types of experiences can provide people with a clearer sense of direction. They point to a path that feels so right that it must have been built especially for you. These experiences illuminate the right road. Some of these experiences reveal the next few steps while others reveal only the very next step.

And speaking of roads, we are reaching a significant point in our journey to understand the nature of callings. We're at a crossroad. While some scientists have discussed callings, they have not identified the source of callings. Jung said it was God. Maslow said it was not. Could it be that callings come from different places for different people? More to the point, we have to ask ourselves: Is there much more that science can tell us about callings?

After an in-depth study of the work of philosopher Søren Kierkegaard and psychoanalyst Otto Rank, Ernest Becker stated, "Both men reached the same conclusion after the most exhaustive psychological quest: that after the very furthest reaches of scientific description, psychology has to give way to 'theology.' "[28] Indeed all of science must eventually give way to theological considerations. This, however, does not detract one iota from the value of science. Science may be the discipline that keeps us from believing too much, while theology is the discipline that keeps us from believing too little.

Achievement

I'm not really talking about success here, at least not in the way people usually mean it. Finding and following one's calling do not always lead to prosperity in the material sense. Your path may never lead to a Nobel Prize or a ticker-tape parade. It may even take you to a place that causes others to shake their heads and whisper about all the great things you could have been.

Callings do not promise to provide financial rewards. In fact, the drive to become a millionaire can be just the thing that keeps you from going where you need to go. Your path may take you to poverty, or it may take you to a destination where money means nothing. Following your calling may never produce a big lottery win or give you the power to impress people or change the world.

One of the best indicators that you are following your path is that you have little need for the material trappings of success. Your accomplishment lies in completing the tasks that have been given only to you. These tasks will not, indeed cannot, be accomplished by anyone else. There is value, then, in a brief discussion of achievement. Specifically, we can learn a great deal about callings by studying people who have achieved much. Within this group we find people tenaciously driven by motives that seem inborn, people who seem pulled by a magnet and pushed by conviction. If we listen closely enough, we can almost hear their callings.

Jean-Paul Sartre believed that "every human being has a project." Thus it becomes the responsibility of each of us to find our particular project, our very purpose. When we do, we release our talents as if they were given to us for the express purpose of completing given projects.

In a study designed to determine why some people become "peak performers" in their professions, psychologist Charles Garfield came to the following conclusion about these extraordinary individuals: "They love most the tasks that embody their deepest values. From those values come missions. And from missions come the tasks that call for the most creative, productive efforts."[29] As Sartre might have said, these stars found their projects. Garfield also comments most interestingly on those instances when gifted workers lose their direction: "I am often asked: 'Do peak performers always have a mission?' No. But when they don't they make finding a mission their mission."[30] Top performers, then, whatever their fields may be, have a deep sense that they have a mission to fulfill. Sometimes the mission may get lost or may change, but there is always a mission nonetheless. They see their challenge as finding and fulfilling their purpose. When they get lost or confused, they are active in the pursuit of their mission.

This is consistent with the teaching of Viktor Frankl, who has insisted that humankind's most fundamental psychological need is to find meaning in life. According to Frankl, we are not meant to sit idly by and ask the question about meaning. In fact, it is not our job to ask that question. Life asks us the question. It is our job to answer it. In other words, the pursuit of our missions is an active one. Passive reflection is not enough. High achievers are aware of this. They search for their projects. For some, it is right in front of them.

Others struggle. Some struggle alone. Others have the support of those who matter most. This support often makes the difference between those who find what they are looking for and those who do not.

It has been said that if Einstein had been born into Mozart's family and Mozart into Einstein's, we would never have heard of either of them. Talent isn't usually enough. In order for talent to blossom, it must grow in the proper soil. It must grow in an environment that appreciates and nurtures it and teaches the young person that his or her gifts have a purpose. Indeed, Mozart was born into a family that cherished music. He was provided with every opportunity to develop his musical nature. If, however, he had grown up in a context that discouraged musical ways, the music might have died. When people find their project, they find courage and energy, but even these noble qualities may not be able to survive a discouraging environment.

Benjamin Bloom, a renowned professor of education at the University of Chicago, has provided ample evidence to support this. He studied 120 extremely talented young adults. His subjects ranged from Olympic swimmers to research neurologists. The aim of his study was to understand how these talented people became so talented and to look for common threads that might connect these exceptional performers. Bloom found that "the parents' special interests were highly related to the field in which one of their children became an outstanding achiever."[31] The formula is not complex. When a child with a particular talent lives in an arena that values that gift, the talent grows. But should that child live in a context that devalues a special talent, it is likely that the talent will not survive.

Developmental psychologist David Feldman has come to the same conclusion. In his research on child prodigies he writes: "One of the myths about prodigies is that their talents are so overwhelming that they will be fulfilled regardless of what happens in their environment. My experience with prodigies makes it clear that precisely the opposite is true."[32] Even extreme talents can get buried. In order to live they must be fed, nurtured, and loved.

The same applies to a person's calling. It can remain stunted, sometimes forever, if it is not encouraged and nurtured. Human beings have a powerful need to be accepted. If our environment will not accept who we really are, we feel a pressure to abandon our true selves and become whatever is needed to be accepted. But there is a price for this. Our callings don't leave us. We can pretend that we can't hear them, but they don't go away. The man who won't be generous because the world he lives in says generosity is foolish will still feel the call to contribute. He just won't let himself answer it. Instead he'll live with feelings of guilt and cowardice. If this condition continues, the guilt and cowardice will become so powerful that it will be difficult to hear what he is being called to do. If he finally loses touch with his calling, all he will be is what other people expect him to be. At this point he has lost his true self.

When people lose touch with their callings, they lose energy and direction. The grief that comes with losing one's mission in life can be devastating. Whether expressed or repressed, anger at those believed responsible for the loss can be extreme. Unlike Garfield's peak performers who make a life of reaching for their missions, those who have lost touch with their projects stop reaching for much of anything. They feel too confused to act on their own.

Many mental health professionals refer to this process as developing a "false self." The false self is an act, a compromise made to please those who judge you. You may appear happy for a time, but eventually a dissatisfaction swells within. You may begin to realize that you want your true self back. If you catch this early enough, the return to genuineness is relatively easy. But if the false self has been given time to solidify, healing can take a long time.

Someone who has built a false self lives with constant confusion. While trying to make important decisions they don't ask themselves, "What do I think is right?" Instead, they have to estimate what their evaluators prefer and ask, "What do *they* want me to do?" An individual with a false self does not take ownership of his or her decisions. In contrast, the souls who keep ownership of their decisions will experience much less confusion. They decide for themselves what is right. This relative lack of confusion is another dimension of high achievers. High achievers tend to have a sharp focus on what they need to accomplish. They let this focus guide and motivate them.

Anne Colby and William Damon, in their research on moral exemplars, recorded that "there was nothing in our knowledge of moral development literature that enabled us to anticipate the exemplars' impervious sense of certainty." They also noted that in spite of this certainty, their subjects still carried a "receptivity toward new ideas and goals." These "moral heroes" could commit themselves to a goal and yet remain open to change.[33]

Dedication does not imply tunnel vision. Dedication means that you have found what is right for you. You have decided to move in this particular direction. Decisions that come from within tend to be the most stable. When we look inside and allow ourselves to discover what is really important, what we feel called to do, then we find a store of certainty and an abundance of energy. With this confidence and energy we are capable of accomplishing much more than we ever could otherwise.

Decisions that come from within do not change on a whim because who we are does not change on a whim. Decisions that are made to please others, however, have little substance. They change with the tide. If we own our decisions, then they will be rooted in our identity, conscience, and spirit. In a sense, we become one with our decisions. Once important decisions are made, changes take place. After the decision comes the commitment and the action. Thought turns to movement, and in the process energy emerges.

German psychologist Heinz Heckhausen has identified what he calls "the Rubicon effect." As the phrase implies, the Rubicon effect describes a single-mindedness of purpose that follows from a commitment to a certain intent (i.e., a mental "crossing of the Rubicon").[34] At this point indecision vanishes as the sense of "there is no turning back" pervades one's being.

A sense of direction combined with a store of energy leads to great achievement, though this success may not be in front of a large and appreciative audience. A person who becomes accomplished in simple kindness and generosity may never receive much acclaim. The farmer may not feel the prestige of the corporate attorney. The carpenter may never know the respect that congressmen take for granted.

The lesson here is that in order to find your calling you have to be prepared to let go of your ego. You must not let others define you. You have your own direction, and it may not lead to wealth and applause. Still, it's your path. It is the most important thing you can do with your life. If you stay on it, you will be rewarded with the energy to travel it well. You will be successful in the area that matters most. You will accomplish your tasks.

One of the best ways to see what it's like to move in a really unique way is to observe creative people. What makes creative people creative? Why do some folks never become creative? Can anyone be creative? What does it take to create something no one else ever has? We don't have all the answers, be we do have a few.

Time and time again creative people speak of having a *vision*. For many this vision begins in childhood. Others acquire it later. It is a look at what needs to be done. It is a glimpse at what is possible. The vision usually communicates that this is not a message meant for everyone. Rather, it presents itself exclusively to a particular individual. Some have suggested that the vision is so personal, so strong, and so moving that it would more accurately be described as a revelation.

In her study of creative geniuses, Denise Shekerjian explains that it is this vision, or revelation, that drives creativity. The extraordinary people who lead the pack are themselves actually following something. After studying forty winners of the coveted MacArthur Foundation Fellowship — sometimes referred to as the "genius award" — she realized that "the examples run on, and in each case it's the *vision* that generates the ideas and carries forth the work, not the hope of praise, reward, or glory."[35]

Visions and revelations are synonymous with callings. The words used don't really matter. The concept, however, is essential to understanding human nature. We maximize our potential by acting on our callings, visions, and revelations. It takes courage to acknowledge them, but when we work through the fear and answer the calling, we are rewarded with the energy necessary to accomplish so much more than we otherwise could. But there are conditions on this gift of energy. If we should decide to ignore our vision, the energy leaves us.

Creative geniuses seem to be among those most loyal to their visions. Even if their visions take them away from the mainstream and they appear aloof or eccentric at times, they go where they need to go. They are more energetic than most and less likely to be distracted. By pursuing their visions they become focused and energized.

Once again, though, we run into the inescapable question: Who or what builds the vision? Who or what is responsible for providing people with their missions? Maybe we can only repeat that science can take us just so far and that we have again reached the point where we must turn our attention to theology. Perhaps we have reached the point where we can only speculate. But before we concede this, I would like to consider one more theory that might be considered within the realm of science.

Even if we cannot yet answer the question of where visions come from, we may be able to understand how people _receive_ their visions. If we can identify where people meet up with their callings, then maybe we are a step closer to finding the source of visions. We can begin by directing this question to creative geniuses. These souls are among the most willing to admit and discuss their visions. Furthermore, they have had the courage and determination to follow the path with heart even while being misunderstood or criticized. In short, they hear a calling and follow it.

What we know is this: (1) highly creative people often begin seeing their visions — hearing their callings — early in life, and (2) they tend to receive them while they are alone. In his book _Solitude,_ Anthony Storr writes:

> Many creative adults have left accounts of childhood feelings of mystical union with Nature; peculiar states of awareness, or "Intimations of Immortality," as Wordsworth called them. Such accounts are furnished by characters as diverse as Walt Whitman, Arthur Koestler, Edmond Gosse, A. L. Rowse, and C. S. Lewis. We can be sure that such moments do not occur when playing football, _but chiefly when the child is on its own._[36]

This brief statement contains two important lessons. First, visions may be more likely to come to us while we are alone. They are frequently born in solitude. They can be better heard when there are fewer sounds and voices to drown them out. Second, a "union with Nature" produces a certain wisdom. It helps banish the clutter in one's mind and teaches one how to hear more than just the noise. It teaches us how to hear the quiet, where the calling is more likely to be.

Nature and solitude: two phenomena that for thousands of years have connected human beings with visions. Religions throughout the ages have recognized the power in nature and solitude. Today millions of people attend retreats to nurture and enrich their spirituality. It's not uncommon for these events to take place away from cities. This is by design. Many people have special spiritual experiences while surrounded by nature. It is common practice for retreats to encourage individuals to spend time by themselves. Strangely enough, at times people need permission before they will spend time alone.

Could it be that they are afraid of what they might realize? The sense of direction and the surge of energy make a calling very attractive, but at some level we know that there is another side to it. What if I'm asked to do something that is beyond me? What if I'm asked to sacrifice? We can avoid these possibilities by avoiding the vision, but this would mean filling our lives with distractions and loud noises. It would mean avoiding quiet time alone for fear of what we might hear and avoiding close contact with nature for fear it might tell us to leave the beaten path and go off on our real journey. If security becomes our sole purpose, reality needs to be distorted.

Maybe this issue comes down to this: If we could identify the exact conditions required for each of us to hear our callings, how many of us would want to know? People receive callings in an open spirit, a spirit willing to listen. Nature and solitude help awaken the spirit, but they are not the only conditions that produce a vision. What is essential is the willingness to see it. This is why children may be more likely to see their visions; they are not as afraid of what they may be called to do.

Conclusion

Callings have led people to great accomplishments. Joan of Arc, Christopher Columbus, Martin Luther King Jr., Charles Lindbergh, and Gandhi — people who altered the course of history — all identified a time in their lives when they felt called upon to fulfill a great mission.[37] Each, in his or her own way, came to recognize the source of this guidance, and all of them followed their callings.

People tend to keep their mail to themselves. We're all entitled to this privacy. So too, most of us keep our visions to ourselves. Again, we're entitled. But the unfortunate consequence of the exercise of this privacy is that the belief in callings has appeared to be without support.

Many great thinkers have described the presence and significance of callings, yet the idea has not gathered great enthusiasm in many circles. This chapter was intended to establish support for the notion of callings. It was about giving people encouragement to believe what they believe. If you believe in callings, you are not alone.

We come to understand our callings in different ways. First and foremost, we learn through our experiences. But we also receive wisdom and guidance from what others are willing to share. If we listen, we can know much that we would otherwise miss.

Picasso once remarked about a painting he had just completed, "It's not what I was searching for — it's what I found." So it is. We do not control all that we are capable of learning. We do not own all that we create. To see a vision or hear a calling we need to let go of the compulsion to control all that we see and hear. When we release this control, we find that life is filled with experiences that move us to the soul. We also come to realize that we are surrounded by masterful teachers. Many people who have allowed themselves to be moved and who have found their callings might agree that Picasso's reflection describes their own situation.

When the vision is found, one may encounter the force that built it. This experience is as personal as the vision itself. Callings, for the most part, have been associated with God. But this matter of the source of callings is something you have to decide for yourself: it's one of those things that no one else can determine for you. It has to be *your* decision, *your* answer, the one *you* find.

Callings Denied

"What did you see, Don Juan?"
"A bunch of nonsense. What else could I have seen without direction?"
> — CARLOS CASTAÑEDA, *The Teachings of Don Juan*

Thus far we have considered the existence of callings. We have addressed what they are and what they mean. We have also looked at the scholarly and scientific support for the belief that we are guided along our own special paths.

Now it's time to deal with an especially crucial issue: Why would someone deliberately try to avoid his or her calling? While no one keeps statistics on this sort of thing, the fact is clear: many, many people turn away from the vision that presents itself specifically and exclusively to them. They pretend they don't see it or hear it. They may pretend so well that they actually lose touch with it. They don't see it as something coming *for* them. Instead, they fear that it is something terrible coming *at* them.

What is the source of this anxiety? To answer this we must remember that fear is almost always rooted in ignorance. In some cases, we fear that which we do not understand; in other cases, we fear that with which we do not know how to deal. For example, children typically fear horses until they begin to understand a horse's ways. And most of us would be frightened by a strange, angry dog if we didn't have the knowledge of how to handle it.

In an age when we are so unwilling to speak the words "callings," "visions," and "revelation," is it really such a mystery that so many of us quake at the door of our greatest awakenings? Where are callings considered an appropriate topic of conversation? You might think that church would be such a place, but I suggest that these discussions are rarely found there. Certainly many faiths *preach* about callings. But where is the discussion? Where is the processing that takes someone else's concepts and makes them your own? A sermon can introduce you to a concept, but you can only come to really accept that concept through dialogue.

In fact, this is how callings are introduced. They are never forced; they are simply suggested, invitations often of the most subtle nature. Once you are introduced, you must be active in your pursuit of that calling. You must move toward a dialogue with your calling. Facing our callings can be quite difficult if we have not even found the time and opportunity to dialogue with others about them. Without this sharing, callings remain mysterious events that can be shrouded in confusion and fear.

Universal and Individual Callings

Everyone actually receives two different (yet related) kinds of callings. We all receive a universal calling, and we all receive an individual calling. The universal calling is usually relatively easy to locate. The individual calling, though, can pose a real challenge.

The universal calling involves contributing to life. We are all called to this. We all have the need to serve. The primary reasons we deny the universal calling are greed and selfishness. The universal calling asks us to give things away — our money, our time, our energy. Although generosity can be a marvelous event that leaves us energized, empowered, and feeling good about ourselves, generosity means sacrifice. Answering the universal calling, then, means you will need to sacrifice. Even so, the universal calling is still often easier to connect with than the individual calling. Chances to contribute to the welfare of human beings, animals, and the environment are plentiful. Any effort on their behalf will do. The universal calling is something we all share, and it asks only that we contribute to life. It is neither hard to find nor hard to follow.

When we find ourselves lost and unable to make sense of our world, the best way for us to reconnect with our purpose is by following the universal calling. It requires little mental energy, and the opportunities are abundant. Alfred Adler made this same suggestion many years ago. He claimed that no one could achieve happiness and mental health until he or she developed a _social interest_. By "social interest" he meant an active involvement in humanity's well-being. People have a basic spiritual and psychological need to give. When we fill this need, our sense of purpose begins to return. I think this is what Karl Menninger meant when he remarked that "generous people are rarely mentally ill."

One of the most important implications of the universal calling is that it makes callings, at least to some extent, very accessible. The universal calling can be heard and answered at any time. Once you understand it, it can seem so obvious that you might wonder how anyone could miss it. Yet it frequently gets overlooked. We can miss our universal calling the same way we miss our opportunities for kindness — because we are too distracted.

Even the most visible kind of calling can be denied. Although we all share the universal calling and it is virtually always within reach, we deny it because it places an obligation on us. This obligation can ultimately produce feelings of strength, confidence, and empowerment; nonetheless, it requires a sacrifice. People unwilling or unaccustomed to sacrifice can have a difficult time with this.

In addition to the universal calling, there is the individual calling. The individual calling is meant specifically for you. It asks that you emerge as an individual to fulfill a mission as only you can. It's all about your uniqueness. It involves acknowledging your uniqueness, then accepting it, and, finally, acting on it. The individual calling is what most people mean when they use the term "calling." It is the answer to the question: What do I need to offer? It can also answer the question: Where do I belong?

While the universal calling asks us to contribute to life, the individual calling asks us to make specific choices, choosing one path over another. The individual calling will not be satisfied through donations to the poor or volunteer work with the needy. Your individual calling asks that you emerge and become your own person. While the universal calling asks for compassion, the individual calling asks for courage. Courage is necessary to develop leadership, creativity, and perseverance. Courage sustains your determination when the ways of the world seem to be obscuring your face and your fingerprints and everything else about you that makes you unique.

Whereas the universal calling speaks a language meant for everyone, the individual calling speaks in a tongue designed for you alone. It introduces itself at its own special time, and it brings a message that has never been given to anyone else. The universal calling is given to us early in life, perhaps at birth. The individual calling can come at any time. Sometimes it waits until we are ready to deal with it. Often it comes when we feel completely unprepared. When the individual calling does arrive, it can be misinterpreted. Mistakes abound. Knowing this, many of us refuse to act on what we believe.

But this is one of the most amazing things about callings: every wrong path has something right about it. Every experience has something to teach. When mistakes are made and you find yourself in a place where you don't belong, you will have to change. Change can be difficult. But before you drag yourself across the coals for that mistake, examine what you have learned. Never put any experience completely behind you. Never waste your experiences.

One of the most fascinating aspects of human behavior is that we are not able to free ourselves from bad experiences until we learn from them. Tragedies cling to us until we determine their lessons. Then we free ourselves. Once we learn what is to be learned, we move on.

Mistakes themselves don't keep people from fulfilling their missions. It's the _fear_ of mistakes that cripples so many of us. We don't move because if we do we might fall down. Or we might move in the wrong direction. We petrify ourselves when we lose sight of the fact that both the fall and the wrong direction have something right about them. This does not remove the need for courage. There will always be a certain amount of anxiety to emerging as your own person. People who do only what they are told may avoid the fear, but they will never know the triumph of building what they have envisioned.

The universal calling and the individual calling are intrinsic to and inherent in each other. The universal calling joins us with the human, animal, and ecological worlds. It is the more basic form of a calling, and the individual calling is built upon (and permanently connected with) it. Should we lose commitment to our universal calling, our individual calling becomes distant and practically inaudible. On the other hand, it is what we become by answering our individual calling that provides us with so much of what we can contribute. The individual calling guides us toward finding out exactly what we need to contribute. By becoming what I am to be, I develop what is needed to make my most important contributions.

From this point forward, when I use the term "calling" (or "vision" or "mission"), I will be speaking of both the individual and the universal callings. They coexist. If we need to address only one of the two, I will make that as clear as possible.

Why We Avoid Our Callings

Within each person's life there is ample opportunity to turn away from one's calling. It can be refused for a while, or it can be denied for an entire lifetime. There is no coercion here. True, there are consequences for walking away from your vision, and a number of these consequences are unpleasant (more on this later). But so too are the sacrifices involved with following one's calling.

We are free to choose. We are free to follow and free to refuse our callings. Many refuse. We could blame this refusal on fear or ignorance. That would, however, be too simple. There are a variety of reasons individuals deny their callings. In the final analysis, someone who turns away from his or her vision has reasons that can only be found within, usually deep within.

We will consider eight reasons people avoid their callings. These obstacles can work alone or they can come in combination. None of them is stronger than the person who carries them. They can all be worked through.

The first and most important step in working through them is to understand them.

Fear

We want to see things in writing before making major commitments. We want the matter spelled out and every imaginable loophole filled. Once all that's taken care of, we buy insurance for protection from the unimaginable. Then we move slowly forward with the assurance that if the floor crumbles beneath us, we can certainly find someone to sue.

We do this to protect ourselves. Big steps are frightening. Take away the guarantees and they can become terrifying. Here's the problem: callings often ask for big steps, and there are no guarantees. You may be asked to walk into the unknown or into a place where you have no support. You may be the one called to slay the dragon, climb the mountain, or walk the wire. It may be your mission to pass through suffering and humiliation.

Abraham Maslow believed this fear to be so common that he gave it a name — the Jonah Complex. He described it as the "evasion of one's own growth, setting low levels of aspiration, the fear of doing what one is capable of doing, voluntary self-crippling." We deny that the mountain is our challenge and settle for nonthreatening molehills. We pretend not to see the dragon that has been placed right in front of us. "We fear our highest possibilities," Maslow wrote. "We are generally afraid to become that which we can glimpse in our most perfect moments, under conditions of great courage."[1]

We move away from our highest possibilities in order to make life safe. Safety is such a devilish tempter. We reduce our lives to ashes through our attempts to possess it. In a life lived to its fullest there is always an element of risk. A thriving being is vulnerable to pain and humiliation. But it is only thriving beings who fulfill the purpose of their lives. It is they who emerge triumphant.

Those who addict themselves to security find themselves in a suit of armor that suffocates their freedom. Their armor imprisons them. "If you deliberately plan to be less than you are capable of becoming," cautioned Maslow, "then I warn you that you'll be deeply unhappy for the rest of your life. You will be evading your own capacities, your own possibilities."[2]

I'm not suggesting that there is no cause for fear. The unpredictability of life is itself cause for anxiety. The unavoidable conclusion that we are all mortal and will someday die adds to the angst. Buy when we add the fact that we have specific tasks that we alone are responsible for, the pressure multiplies. With this added responsibility comes a fear of failure, and this fear may be the most common reason that people deny their callings. It's not for lack of evidence as much as it is fear. Fear that I could try and fail. Fear that with such a failure I may become unacceptable to the force that sends our callings. For many this means failure in the eyes of God.

The fear that one has interpreted one's calling incorrectly — the fear of traveling in the wrong direction — is, like the fear of failure, based in feelings of inadequacy. I won't get it right. I can't trust my judgment. Everything I do turns out wrong. These are beliefs that build walls of fear between you and your vision.

Although there is cause for anxiety, there is no reason to retreat behind a fortress of denial. If we allow ourselves to experience our callings, we will find all the spirit we need to accomplish our tasks. As I discussed earlier, callings provide courage. This certainly does not mean that a calling rids us of all our fear. Fear is a part of a full life. Furthermore, courage should not be confused with fearlessness. Courage is the force that helps us walk through fear.

Unfortunately, many people let the fear of fear keep them from getting close enough to their callings. Hence they don't receive the courage needed to follow their callings. If they never touch the power, they will never become empowered.

Shame

Once someone reaches the conclusion "I can't get there from here," there is a good chance that that person will turn away from her or his destination and ask: "Why go on? Why wander about foolishly without hope? What would be the purpose? If I pursue this calling, won't my fate be as humiliating as the rest of my life? How can I expect more?"

The relationship between shame and the denial of callings is a bit more complex than it may seem at first. Shame affects one's journey in two ways. First, certain people feel too ashamed of themselves to fulfill their callings. They see what needs to be done, and they feel the internal pull to make their contribution in a particular area. Still, they convince themselves that they are too helpless or ineffective to get the job done. They lack confidence in their abilities. They hear their callings but sit back with their rationalizations for why they can't do what they are called to do.

Second, some people are ashamed of their callings. What arrived wasn't what they had hoped for. A young man, for instance, may have grown up with the hope of becoming a policeman. He felt good as he saw himself in a very masculine and honorable role. As time passes, however, a small spark turns into a burning desire to teach young children. He keeps this vision to himself because he doesn't feel an elementary school teacher is a proper vocation for a man. But the vision continues. He thinks how much easier life would have been if he had not been called to guide young children. He can still be a police officer, but this work will never take him where he needs to be. He needs to be a teacher. This may not be the easy way or the proud way, but this is what is. In the process of deciding whether to accept or refuse his calling, he must ask himself, "Can I accept this mission? Can I accept who I am?"

Shame can affect us in either or both ways. We can be ashamed of ourselves, our callings, or both. If we are ashamed of ourselves, we tend to wear disguises that prevent others from seeing who we really are. People who are ashamed of themselves live with the belief that if others knew them as they really are, they would be rejected. On the other hand, if we are ashamed of our callings, we also try to pretend. We pretend we are happy. The appearance of happiness can be a way of disguising one's shame. I wear the disguise and hope that if I pretend well enough, maybe my calling will change to something that is easier to accept.

Popeye knew how to deal with this. When things reached their worst and he felt totally victimized, he empowered himself with his famous cry, "I am what I am and that's all that I am!" As he shouted this for the world to hear, he became strong, determined, courageous, invincible. Once he professed that what he was, no matter how flawed, was good enough, his flaws became insignificant. He could then conquer his persecutor.

Shame, the feeling of being inadequate, is a lie. It is always a lie. But it can rule our lives until we see our lives as a lie. There is tremendous value in every person and in every calling. Sometimes, like Popeye, we have to scream this before we start believing it. We begin to shed our shame when we start taking ownership of our self-evaluation. If you refuse to accept the shame that others attempt to place upon you, you will free yourself.

Mythologist Joseph Campbell was quite correct when he

told interviewer Bill Moyers, "The world is full of people who have stopped listening to themselves or have listened only to their neighbors to learn what they ought to do, how they ought to behave, and what the values are that they should be living for."[3] If you follow shame to its source you'll find it comes from somebody else. You become ashamed of yourself when someone important to you judges you to be unimportant and you accept this verdict. Once shame sets in, it creates so much confusion that how it was acquired gets lost. How to release it can get muddled as well. Shame defeats you before you begin. Although it is a lie, if you let it, it can be a powerful and destructive lie. It denies the value that is intrinsic within you and the value and worth inherent in your calling.

In recent years our culture has focused on and learned much about shame and how it affects people. We have not, however, given sufficient thought to how and why we become ashamed of our callings. One of the ways we, as a culture, shame a calling is by taking away respect. Carpentry, for instance, is a wonderful calling. A good carpenter is a craftsman and a contributor to the community. But in most cases a carpenter will not receive the prestige of a rocket scientist. A doctor usually receives more prestige than a teacher. A teacher tends to get more respect than a plumber. As a society we give more value to some callings than we do to others. We glorify some callings and shame others.

Again, shame is a lie: all callings are equal. There are many right paths, and not one of these paths is better than any other. What matters is that you walk *your* path. You may have to walk past condemning eyes. This doesn't change a thing. You do what you are to do and keep your head up. No one has a calling more wonderful than your calling.

Abandonment

People are sometimes called to new environments. Some must travel far away to find where they belong. Some do not move very far at all and yet end up in a whole new world. When you move to answer your calling, you may fear that those closest to you will not be able or willing to accept your decisions. Sometimes this fear is groundless and you find that, ultimately, those who mean the most to you remain loyal and supportive. But the endings are not all happy. There are occasions when people must choose between their loved ones and the life they feel is calling them. In some cases the abandonment is temporary, an adjustment period. Sometimes the abandonment is forever: spouses walk out; friends say goodbye; family members disown each other. If we lose those closest to us, our world changes. We may wonder if anything could be worth this sacrifice.

The blessing of hearing one's calling can become pure torment in such situations. People become torn between two powerful needs — the need for people and the need to be who they really are. Unfortunately, many callings are lost in this dilemma, and this points to how important support is. Children grow up happier and healthier if their parents surround them with unconditional love. These children know they will be loved no matter what. And when it comes time to choose the roads they will travel in life, they are not risking their parents' love and support. Children raised in contexts like this are free to seek and act on their visions. It is all right to be their own person.

In healthy families people are allowed to have their own directions. They don't have to follow in the footsteps of father or grandfather. They are encouraged to have their own dreams. If the support and encouragement are unconditional and remain in place, then children grow into adults who will not be abandoned while they pursue their callings. Their base is solid, and they can focus their attention on their mission.

If, however, the support disappears, the road becomes frightening. Often this conflict rages on at an unconscious level, with people being unaware of the cause for their turmoil. Once they come to the understanding that their pain exists because they do not have the support to do what they need to do, they can address it head-on. Those who look this conflict straight in the face often come to the awakening that love that keeps them from their calling is not healthy love. Finding your vision, then, can mean leaving unhealthy love and finding healthy love.

Ignorance

Noted psychiatrist and author Eric Berne once remarked, "If no radio is heard in someone's house, that does not mean he lacks one; he may have a good one, but it needs to be turned on and warmed up before it can be heard clearly." If we took this metaphor a step further, we might add that everyone has a good radio even though some don't realize that they have one at all. Before the radio can be found, turned on, warmed up, and heard clearly, the owner must understand that it's there.

Many (perhaps most) people in our day and age have never thought of having a calling. They've never heard it taught. And even if they have heard it taught, they've never heard it valued. Many believe in a calling in the same way they believe in Adam and Eve or Noah's Ark — that it is symbolic, at best. It gets dumped way back in the mind in the burial ground for disregarded beliefs.

Without an understanding of callings, however, life can be very confusing, since callings come to you whether you believe in them or not. If you understand what they are, you will be more likely to hear them clearly. There will be less fear and uncertainty. If, on the other hand, you know nothing about callings, they can be unsettling. Their pull can feel like an impending mental illness — as if you might be losing control, as if you are being torn apart.

If you move with your calling, you will be guided by a beneficent force. If you fight it, you will feel lost, confused, and possibly out of control. We could say this is like swimming in a river. If you swim with the current, there is no feeling of being assaulted or conquered. But if you try to swim against the current, you fight a force more powerful than you. If you move with the current, you are in harmony with the forces that command the river. Your movement will be so natural that you may lose awareness that the current exists. The current becomes a part of you. You become one with nature. If you swim against the stream, it feels destructive. You and nature will be at odds, and it will take all your energy to make minimal progress. No energy. No harmony. No triumph.

Furthermore, if you don't understand the current, then the river can be thoroughly overwhelming. A movement in one direction feels right. Another movement, this time in a different direction, feels wrong. And you won't know why. It takes an understanding of the river and its current to comprehend why some movements feel right and others seem all wrong, why some moves are empowering and others self-defeating. Callings, it seems, are a lot like rivers.

The Need for Control

People tend to like control. We enjoy swimming in the river as long as we have more control than the river. When the water generates more power than we have, things start to get frightening.

Members of Alcoholics Anonymous have a piece of advice they like to share: "Let go and let God." This simple wisdom is about letting go of your need to control every aspect of your life. It suggests that we should allow ourselves to be moved by a force more powerful than ourselves. It means we should trust the ways of our Higher Power.

Releasing the need for complete control frees us. It frees all the energy that it takes to hold on to certainty. With this surge of energy we are capable of accomplishing more than we ever could; we are capable of surviving in new territories. When we let go of certainty and security, we allow life to not only teach us but also pull us in the direction we need to go. We become spontaneous and growing beings.

Many times when people finally let go they find that they are led back to the spot where they began. In other words, they were exactly where they belonged all the time. But there is a difference. After freeing themselves from the need to control everything about their lives, they can find more than the place where they want to be — they can find the place where they belong. This can occur only to those who will let themselves be called.

Carl Jung once wrote, "Most of my patients knew the deeper truth but did not live it. And why did they not live it? Because of the bias which makes us all put the ego in the center of our lives."[4] Jung could just as well have said, "We want things our way and we don't want to risk the chance that they might turn out differently." What is especially interesting about his observation is the insight that most of his patients "knew the deeper truth but did not live it." The implication here is that no matter how much we may deny it in our efforts to maintain control, at some level we realize that by trying to completely control our destinies, we lose our lives.

If we permit our callings to direct us, we may end up somewhere that, at this moment, we do not want to go. More often, though, this is just a rationalization for refusing to let go. A calling will take you to the place where you belong. True, you may face hardship along the way, but you will always arrive at the place where you belong.

Besides the fear that we could end up in a bad place, there is a second worry. Some people believe that if they let go of what they have and where they are now, they will never find anything of value and will spend their lives lost. To an extent, this is a valid fear. More than one soul has found itself lost on the way to achieving its vision. What people often fail to realize, however, is that getting lost is a crucial part of many callings. It may be what you find while you are lost that enables you to answer your calling. Robert Frost may have said it best when he suggested that you need to become "lost enough to find yourself."

The trouble is, we don't like being lost. We want to be in control, and when we are lost, we feel out of control. We don't like letting go and letting God because this means surrendering control. Many of us tell ourselves that we are handing our lives over to God when this really isn't so. What we may mean by God is just another name for ourselves. I think Princeton psychologist Julian Jaynes was right when he claimed, "In a sense, we have become our own gods."[5] If we become our own gods, then we don't have to let go of anything.

In order to live your callings you must be prepared to surrender some of your control. You must let yourself wander and dream. You can keep your feet on the ground and maintain your good judgment and still open yourself up to a force greater than yourself. You may call this force God, nature, the universe, or any other name. But you can know it only by following it. It will care for you. Even when it asks you to sacrifice, it will care for you.

A calling will have a difficult time reaching you clearly if you will not open yourself to receiving it. A revelation may unsettle you. Callings come most directly to people who allow themselves to be a bit unsettled.

Greed

Greed is a failed attempt at control. It drives people to try to acquire things that they believe will protect them from what they fear. For instance, individuals hoard money for the purpose of protecting themselves from insufficiency — but that rarely leads to their losing that fear of want. They just become wealthier people who continue to fear.

Because greedy people spend so much of their time and energy pursuing control, they have real trouble hearing their callings. And if they do hear them, they are too involved with their greed to accept what they are called to do. This is one of the reasons greedy people are so angry. They distance themselves from who they are and where they need to be. In the end, greed forces people to lose control of their lives. Greed is a retreat from one's destiny.

Maybe the biggest problem with greed is that there is a lock on it. When greedy people feel tormented by their greed, they don't usually change their ways. Rather, they do more of the same; they get greedier. Their solution to their torment becomes their problem. This is why greedy people are so mean-spirited; their attempts at control are self-destructive.

It's important to note that strife can strike the rich and the poor. Wealth is not the issue here. Greed is. Greed exists in all socioeconomic classes, and I don't know if one class has more of it than any other. Greed is more about attitudes than incomes. It's an attitude that keeps people from seeing their visions. Beyond the fact that greed distances individuals from their callings, there is a second concern. Greed is a direct violation of the universal calling — the calling to contribute to life. As discussed above, we are all called to this. No matter what our individual callings may be, we are all called to be caregivers to the life (be it human, animal, or plant) that surrounds us.

Another aspect of greed's preventing us from fulfilling the most fundamental aspect of our callings has to do with the fact that many people begin to fulfill their callings by addressing the universal calling. If the universal calling is not satisfied, they may never even approach their individual callings. Greed, then, can cripple us from the beginning. If it is not reversed, through compassion and generosity, one's calling may never be answered, and that soul may never know anything more than bitterness and resentment.

Intellectualizing

Some people think too much. Whatever the subject, they break it down, disassemble it, weigh it, measure it, categorize it, and then discuss it. Even their ideas and beliefs are dissected this way. People who think too much prefer complicated beliefs, ones that can be analyzed endlessly. In fact, this is (unfortunately) how they select their beliefs. They look for notions that feed their compulsion to think. They believe that thinking is more important than truth.

Overly intellectual persons miss a lot. They see the pieces but not the whole. In *The Tao of Pooh,* Benjamin Hoff explains that "the surest way to become Tense, Awkward, and Confused is to develop a mind that tries too hard — one that thinks too much."[6] The tension, awkwardness, and confusion are not sicknesses as much as they are *signs,* signs that one is doing something wrong. If life gets too complex, maybe it's time to return to simplicity. Emerson put it perfectly: "Let the bird sing without deciphering the song."

Besides the headaches and confusion, too much thought can produce another problem — paralysis, inactivity. Regrettably, some folks are all thought and no action. You can think yourself into quicksand. Considering all the possibilities, consequences, and ramifications can take more than a lifetime. Thought without action is as useless as action without thought is dangerous. A calling always asks for more than thought. It asks for movement. Certainly thought is a necessary component of effective action. But thought has no purpose without movement. It is not enough to understand one's vision. A vision will never be fulfilled until it is acted upon.

We can rationalize cowardice. If we are afraid to move, we can come up with a thousand reasons to remain motionless. The argument against action can be persuasive. After all, it's probably safer not to step onto the field, out into traffic, or up to the microphone. Too much risk. And there are so many intelligent-sounding reasons not to risk.

Thus, people who think too much tend not to connect with their callings. Their demand for complexity as well as their unwillingness to act keep them far from where they are meant to be. Complicating matters is the reality that callings don't always point themselves completely at the brain. Callings are often first heard through one's feelings. They tug at the emotions. Since compulsive thinkers spend little time with their emotions, they miss these opportunities to discover where they belong.

Sometimes the best way to touch your callings is to ask yourself, "What do I love?" If you allow yourself to love and if you can honestly and courageously answer this, you may begin to realize your vision. People who think too much, however, struggle with love. Love is too simple to be analyzed thoroughly. It's not logical that such important answers can be found through feelings. So they sit in the quicksand and think — and sink.

Refusing to Believe

"In order to take control of our lives and accomplish something of lasting value," says Benjamin Hoff, "sooner or later we need to learn to Believe."[7] We need to learn to believe more than what we can see, hear, feel, taste, and touch. What we see, hear, feel, taste, and touch can never provide enough direction or passion in anyone's life. There is more to it. We have to believe in a big picture — a picture that can be understood only by those with more than five senses.

The trouble is this: the five senses produce information that can be rather easily validated. It doesn't take a great deal of courage to believe what everyone else can see with their eyes and hear with their ears. It's the material we gather through our other sense that can be difficult, and sometimes impossible, to explain to others. This is key. You have to be brave to believe in something all by yourself.

People who refuse to believe do so for any number of reasons. More than anything else, they don't want to take the chance that they may be believing something by themselves. They have little desire for private beliefs. They feel private beliefs are too frightening. Callings are undesirable to them because a calling is a very private belief. It points to a singular mission or set of missions.

To understand how difficult it can be to believe in something when no one else does, consider the following: if no one else believed in love, could you? If no one else believed in God, could you? If no one else believed in a soul or an afterlife, could you? If no one around you believed in a calling, could you? You can fill in any belief you hold sacred. Then ask yourself if you could hold it at all if no one else did.

No one is asking you to give up your shared beliefs: they can be beautiful and life-giving. They can give you love and support. But they will not give you enough direction. In order to find your own path you must be willing to believe in a message meant only for you. If you have the courage to believe when no one else does, then you have the courage to live your calling. This courage begins in a willingness to believe.

There are other reasons people avoid their callings. We have considered eight: fear, shame, abandonment, ignorance, the need for control, greed, intellectualizing, and refusing to believe. Any of these reasons may work alone or in combination with the others. In fact, people are always inventing new reasons to avoid the responsibility of a calling.

Besides all the reasons people use to deny a calling, there is also a myth that has kept many a soul from reaching its vision. Many people who are sincerely willing to be called miss their callings when they think that callings wait to arrive until they are ready to receive them. They assume that callings don't speak until their lives are stable, secure, and they are prepared to commit themselves to do whatever they are asked.

The fact is that callings ask beggars to be generous and children to change the world. Someone in the midst of cancer treatment may hear a calling to become a physician. A city dweller may be called to farming or forestry, and a learning disabled child may be called to be another Einstein (who himself was learning disabled). During the worst time in your life you may be called to make your greatest contribution.

You calling doesn't wait until you are a finished product (whatever that might be). Your calling comes to you, and you must grow toward it. I don't know if anyone is ever really ready for a calling. The calling, if you accept it, helps make you ready. But what if you do not accept it? What happens if you deny your visions? We have considered why people refuse their callings. Now we must estimate the cost.

The Cost of Denial

When we talk about the costs that accompany the denial of a calling, we have to take into account two different types of costs. The first, and more difficult to discern, is the cost to humanity. Does humankind suffer because a single individual does not fulfill her or his mission? Does it affect anyone else besides Jane Doe if she does not fulfill her calling? Second, what are the consequences to the individual? In other words, what happens to Jane Doe should she turn away from her vision?

We can state confidently that if someone does not fulfill her or his universal calling to contribute, then at some level the world will feel the effects of this. But what about the individual calling? Does it matter to anyone else but me whether I become a farmer or a teacher? As long as I fulfill my obligation to humankind, how is it anyone else's business what I do with my life? This is a difficult yet important question. We don't know why people are called to do what they are called to do. Consequently, we don't know for sure how necessary it is, from a global perspective, for us to follow the spirit that guides us. The only way we could possibly answer this question would be to step back and observe humanity from a metaperspective. We would need a perch from which to observe how our behavior impacts our entire world, present and future. Only then could we begin to know if and why others need us to be what we are called to be. Since we have no such perch, we may never know how important our individual calling is to the history of the world.

But in spite of the fact that we cannot prove that the universe needs each of us to follow our individual callings, there are indications that *we* need to fulfill these callings. It's as if at some level we understand that which we cannot prove. We know that our callings need to be answered and that failure to do so is more than a personal choice. Somehow this refusal has consequences far and wide and for years to come. Within our beings we feel an obligation to become what only we can be. This is an obligation to one's self and to all of humankind.

I don't know why some are called to be healers and others to be craftsmen. I do know, however, that people who refuse their callings live with the guilt of having turned their backs on humanity. This response is so common that it lends proof to the hypothesis that everyone's individual calling has a special place in the development of a better world. It's as if deep inside us we have a conviction that says that for the sake of the universe, we need to be what we need to be, even though we can't always understand why.

So what are the consequences for refusing your direction? Actually, we have already found one. People who deny their callings tend to have rather shallow interpersonal relationships. They know, sometimes unconsciously, that they are not performing the tasks that would link them most securely and passionately to the rest of humankind. Callings join people. In fact, one of the clearest signals that one has turned away from one's calling is an inability to connect with others. Even when surrounded by people, a loneliness remains.

This supports the contention that humankind needs everyone's mission. Although we are not able to see just how everyone's work fits together (i.e., we don't have that perch), we can see how people who find their tasks feel much more included in the development of humanity. We can carefully conclude that the world loses something each time someone denies a calling. With our callings comes an obligation. We feel obliged to give our piece to the survival of human life and the human spirit, no matter how insignificant our work may seem at the time. If we could stay on the perch that would allow us to see how it all fits together, I think we would see that the universe needs every piece of art that has ever been created and every single garden that has ever been grown.

All human beings are free to refuse the work that is sent them. A person can attempt to create whatever destiny she or he chooses. What I have been suggesting, however, is that during our lives we each receive a certain set of special requests. These callings ask us to accomplish certain things with our lives, and a powerful guilt lives inside those who deny these callings. Guilt is the grumbling that can roll and thunder through our beings. When we move away from what we are meant to be we feel remorse that can be corrected only by changing paths.

The guilt manifests itself in many ways. It can look like depression or hostility. Sometimes it masks itself with an addiction. At other times it presents itself as a disgruntled grandiosity. If the guilt becomes so loud that it clouds a person's reason, it can lead to suicide. The guilt can be the foundation of virtually any form of emotional pain. The expression can be as unique as the individual. We must remember, though, that the form of expression is not the real problem. The pain will not go away until one removes the guilt.

The type of guilt we are talking about here represents, as Ernest Becker once wrote, "the failure to live one's own life."[8] If this situation is allowed to continue there is a marked deterioration of the psyche and spirit. The guilt doesn't go away by itself. It persists until the person changes the direction of his or her life. As it persists it covers its tracks in a way that makes it hard to identify just where it came from. Confusion frequently accompanies the guilt.

Then, as mentioned earlier, there is the energy drain that comes from repressing one's calling. In the early stages when one's calling is barely audible, little energy is required to repress it. But as the volume increases, so does the energy needed to bury it. This escalation can continue until the majority of an individual's psychic and spiritual energies are being spent in the service of denial. All this energy that could be used for creativity, building relationships, achievement, work, love, and humor is wasted in the process of refusing to live one's own life.

A client I once treated exemplifies rather well how painful this condition can become as well as what must occur to make the appropriate corrections. I'll call him Paul (not his real name). Paul was a successful business executive in his late thirties. Married with three young children, he appeared to personify the American dream. His family was healthy; he had what seemed to be a bright future; and he had just about all the material possessions anyone could want. No one questioned whether Paul was happy. Everyone who knew him assumed that he ought to be happy, so no one looked any further.

Although he and his wife kept it a very tight secret, their marriage was falling apart. His wife made vague demands on him such as, "I need to know how you _really_ feel, and I don't know who you are." Although an intelligent man, Paul had a block on issues like these. He couldn't (or wouldn't) understand what she meant.

While Paul appeared contented to his friends and distant to his wife, he was an awfully sad man. He had a number of explanations as to why he kept his misery hidden (e.g., "the kids," his boss, co-workers, etc.), so he kept it all to himself. Even to himself it appeared that he had everything that makes men his age happy. This added to his confusion. As time passed Paul began to feel that there would be no solution and that his present condition would be his fate. With no savior in sight, he decided to kill himself.

No one knew he owned a gun. Another secret. He removed the pistol from his closet and placed it on the desk in his bedroom. Then as his final act he started to scribble a suicide note. In the note he intended to leave an explanation for what he was about to do. He quickly found that a note was not enough. The note turned into a short letter, then a long one. The letter gradually turned into an autobiography. He began to expose his unexamined life and became moved by what he found.

A line from John Greenleaf Whittier's poem "Maud Muller" reads: "For of all sad words of tongue or pen, the saddest are these: It might have been." As Paul read what began as a suicide note he realized that his life to date had been one big "it might have been." He identified things he had avoided, important things. Most importantly, he realized that the life he intended to end was not the life he was supposed to be living. What he really wanted to do was kill a false self and free himself from guilt and confusion.

By the time Paul came to see me he was already well on the road to recovery. He had begun to see what was real. With this clearer vision came a growing energy. He now had the vitality and desire to look at himself and his life to find where he really belonged.

It didn't take long. During our second session he told me how he loved the mountains. He had spent time there in his youth, and while he enjoyed every minute of it, until now he never thought that this might be where he needed to be. He then spoke of a second revelation. He told me he had always wanted to work with children. He wasn't quite sure in exactly what capacity, but he was getting in touch with a deep need to teach children. Maybe as a school teacher, maybe as a coach. He didn't know how, but he did know he wanted to work with kids. As he told me this a thought crossed my mind. I wondered if he needed to go to the mountains to hear the rest of his mission. His calling might become clearer there. He had some ideas about what it involved (i.e., children), but he needed more. I wondered if he were being called to the place where the vision would emerge.

Emergence best described Paul's awakening. His suicidal moment put him in touch with who he really was. This revelation occurred at the point when no one else's opinion mattered. He felt, perhaps for the first time, free. He was free to hear the messages that were meant especially for him.

As with all stories about callings, this one has no real ending. I saw Paul for six sessions. The thoughts of suicide had left him. Not only did he want to live, he now had something to live for, to fulfill, to complete. Whether or not he made it to the mountains I may never know. I had the privilege of watching him open the door to his calling. He loved what he saw. When I think about Paul I hope that he walked through that door.

Paul's experience is not unusual. People often get completely lost before they find where they belong. The poet Theodore Roethke knew that "in a dark time, the eye begins to see." As mentioned above, Robert Frost suggested that we must lose ourselves before we can find ourselves. Once we find ourselves and our eyes begin to see, we become clearer of mind and more energetic. We become more resilient. When we are in our callings, we are stronger and more immune to stress. When we are away from our callings, we are more vulnerable to stress. Our psychological immune system deteriorates when we lose our correct path.

We live in a day and age when health-care professionals are quick to diagnose their patients as sick when they are not. Instead, they may be lost. If you treat people as if they are sick, you can mortally wound their spirits. Being lost is an opportunity. The fact that someone is lost indicates that he or she is willing to wander and explore. These qualities are tremendously valuable in the search for one's mission. Getting lost is not sick. Assuredly, getting lost is more often an act of courage.

Those *not* willing to risk getting lost are more appropriately described as sick. They suffer from a wide variety of afflictions including guilt, loneliness, self-destructiveness, confusion, lowered immunity to stress, and a lack of energy. Those who refuse their callings never find the contentment that life can provide. They never find the focus and direction that come with dedicating themselves to a cause that is greater than they are. They never feel the empowerment that comes with being asked to improve the world in a way that only they can.

One of the greatest tragedies of our age is the human suffering that continues unabated because we are reluctant to consider a missing calling as its cause. We don't see it because we don't want to look at it. Our age, which is so in love with its freedom and choice, sees a calling as a threat to our precious freedom. We love the notion that we can be anything we want. But all this imagined potential has caused great pain. I'm sorry, but we can't be anything and everything we want to be. We all have limitations. And we all have our missions. Until we understand this many souls will live in needless torment.

In other times religion and the church gave support, encouragement, and direction to those who had lost their callings. Sadly, this has changed. Religion has become a method to help people gain control. The idea of "thy will be done" has been replaced with "please, Lord, help me control my world." Surrender and prayer for direction have been replaced with a plea (and expectations) for control.

In his book *Simply Sane,* psychiatrist Gerald G. May describes the situation this way:

> Religion has changed. What had been a way of calling people's consciousness back to their roots has now become a way of trying to insure a good harvest.... Now people try to control the gods.... Religion, once a way of listening to the voice of sanity, has fallen prey to the insatiable will of human beings to do and to control. Religion has been transformed into superstition.[9]

We have made religion fit our age. We've also done this with education and mental health care. We don't look for direction — we look for control. As I have said repeatedly, acknowledging the existence of a calling threatens our control. It's as if we need to believe that we choose our fate and that fate could not possibly choose us.

We don't select our callings. We can't exchange them. We can't control them. We can refuse them, but there are costs for doing so. We live in a time of disregarded callings. Thus we live in an age of guilt, loneliness, confusion, and self-destructiveness.

We achieve our true potential only when we accept that there are limits to our potential. There are limits to our choices. A calling is a limitation. It is a mission that can give you great happiness. But it is not something you ask for. It chooses you.

Chapter Four

Callings Found

If one advances confidently in the direction of his dreams, and endeavors to live the life which he has imagined, he will meet with a success unexpected in common hours. He will put something behind and will pass an invisible boundary.

— HENRY DAVID THOREAU

People connect with their callings in a variety of ways. To some they arrive gradually, perhaps so gradually that there is no identifiable event when and where the connection takes place. This process is sometimes referred to as a gradual awakening, and it can be so subtle that people who have lived through the process may not even understand terms like "callings" and "visions." A gradual awakening can be so smooth that it is virtually unconscious. That is, people going through the process have little conscious understanding that they are following anything at all. Their callings never have to shout so loud as to call attention to themselves. These souls are so attuned to their callings that they feel one with them.

Many of us, however, know (at least at some point in our lives) the confusion that comes from not knowing where we belong. This is the feeling that something is missing, something important. The void can make us miserable. It's a wound that won't heal, a hunger that burns, a dull lingering ache or a sharp piercing pain that won't lift until we find our direction. The wise old Dr. Seuss put it simply when he wrote to everyone, "Your mountain is waiting." We cannot find peace until we find our mountain, the one we need to climb.

Absence makes the heart more aware. We learn a lot about the nature of a vision when we have lost our own. Discomfort brings its own brand of insight and its own kind of appreciation. Being unable to find our callings can teach us a lot about callings. Among other things, it makes us grateful when our calling begins to emerge. Gratitude is often the first step in the process of accepting a calling. It is also a quality that pervades a life that is true to its vision.

When a calling emerges and is met with gratitude, changes begin, powerful changes. Angst turns into energy. Confusion disappears. Guilt melts away. It's not so much that people become instantly secure, but, at the very least, they no longer have any inclination to dwell on whatever insecurity may remain. People don't become perfect as they meet their callings, and not all of their problems go away. They do, however, become psychologically healthier and more spiritually alive.

The psychiatrist Roberto Assagioli described the spiritual awakening this way:

> The harmonious inner awakening is characterized by a sense of joy and mental illumination that brings with it an insight into the meaning and purpose of life; it dispels many doubts, offers the solution to many problems and gives an inner source of security. At the same time there wells up a realization that life is one, and an outpouring of love flows through the awakening individual towards his fellow beings and the whole of creation. The former

personality, with its sharp edges and disagreeable traits, seems to have receded into the background and a new loving and lovable individual smiles at us and the whole world, eager to be kind, to serve, and to share his newly acquired spiritual riches, the abundance of which seems to him almost too much to contain.[1]

Visions can be found in a series of small quiet moments, in what Abraham Maslow called peak-experiences, in what Albert Bandura calls chance encounters, or in the sudden explosions that Assagioli refers to as harmonious inner awakenings. A calling can begin to emerge at any time through virtually any event.

I once heard a missionary tell a most interesting little story. He said that when he was in his midtwenties he was living with his parents and floundering without a direction in life. One day the mail brought a request for a donation to the missions, the kind of request that had come to his house many times before. This time, though, was different. He didn't throw it away or dismiss it with a small donation. He read it. And then read it again. And again. And again. To make a long story short: he donated himself. He became a missionary and found a life of much joy, contentment, and meaning. The moral of the story, he claimed, relates to the letter he received requesting a donation: "I guess one man's junk mail can be another man's calling." In this case, a routine experience (i.e., a request for a donation) touched something deep within this man and touched off the kind of experience that Assagioli spoke of. Part of his calling came from within; the other piece came through the mail.

This experience is not uncommon. An external event (which often appears accidental) pollinates an internal force. That internal force then begins to blossom in a way so deliberate and natural that it seems to have been waiting for the opportunity to come alive. At first these experiences look accidental. In hindsight, and upon examination, they appear inevitable.

In order for this process to unfold we must be willing to look within. When we feel ourselves react strangely to a new experience or even one we have encountered a thousand times before, we have to ask ourselves, Why? What is it about this experience that I need to know? What is it asking me? What is it telling me? Sometimes people are afraid to ask these questions because they fear being called to do something that may frighten them. This is a reasonable and very human fear. Most of us have some fear of the unknown. What many fail to consciously realize is that much of what is inside us is unknown. We shy away from looking within ourselves for fear of what we may find, but to see our visions we have to overcome that fear.

There is a fascinating Native American tale that explains this situation in its own special way. At the beginning of time, the story goes, three spirits roamed the earth, and these three spirits held the secret to life. They knew that humans would soon inhabit the land. But they could not decide how to pass on the secret to life. Finally, the three agreed that the lesson should be given only to those of solid character, people with strength and valor. So they agreed that they would put the secret in a place that could be reached only by persons with these qualities. One spirit suggested that it be placed on top of the highest mountain. Another spirit recommended the bottom of the deepest ocean. The third spirit (the wisest) disagreed. She said that the secret to life should be placed deep inside each human being. She knew that only the most courageous would be willing to look for it there. The other spirits agreed immediately. And so it is to this very day that the secret to life remains where the spirits first placed it, deep within each of us.

Where do we get the courage to look into the unknown? A plethora of answers have been offered over the years. Some thinkers have proposed that courage is an inherent dimension of the human condition, a natural phenomenon. Others have maintained that it is not an inborn quality and that in order to possess courage we must be taught it. Then there are other beliefs such as that advanced by Socrates, who said that courage is "neither natural nor taught" but comes to us "by divine dispensation."[2]

I suspect this is one of those important issues that people must answer for themselves. Where do you get your courage? Some will agree with Socrates and say they get their courage from God. Others will tell you they get it from rubbing their rabbit's foot. Others will say they don't know. The most courageous people, though, are those who have the most direct path to the greatest supply of courage.

Something I have said a number of times before bears repeating here: every calling comes with the courage needed to fulfill it. Those who decide to look for their visions and courage and then move to create the things they are asked walk through fear to a life with direction, purpose, and effectiveness. They reach a serenity known only to those who have traveled this road.

Describing all the ways people hear their callings would take up a separate and long book. In what follows, then, I want to discuss just three common stages involved in connecting with a calling. The first is the exploration stage. Here a person looks around and learns about life. Next comes the action stage, where an individual moves into his or her own arena. Finally, there is the mentoring stage, where the lessons that have been learned are passed on to those in their exploration stage.

We learn. We do. We educate.

The Stages of a Calling

Some people have callings that are focused on one specific area. Others are called to a variety of arenas. There are folks who search long and hard before finding their missions. Then there are those who just stumble upon them.

The single most common reason people miss their callings is that they don't believe in them. A calling is much harder to hear when you refuse to believe in it. You probably won't let yourself see your vision if you insist that visions don't exist. And though some callings scream so loud that even the most determined skeptic becomes a believer, too many callings are missed for no other reason than the unwillingness to believe.

You don't have to be convinced that there are callings in order to hear one. Your chances of connecting with your calling, however, greatly improve if you at least accept the *possibility* that they are real. You're then more likely to look, listen, and feel when a particular experience seems to be sending you a message. Those who are open, consciously or unconsciously, to the voice of a calling begin their journey in the exploration stage.

The Exploration Stage

We enter the world with a strong, vibrant curiosity. We know, of course, that curiosity is the desire to learn, but there is more to it. Curiosity is a form of love. It's an expression of love for our world.

Strangely, although we all begin life with an active curiosity, we are not all curious about the same things. One person discovers a fascination with mechanical things while her twin brother becomes enthralled with teaching. She feels a special concern for the welfare of the environment while he is moved more deeply by the tragedy of child abuse. Two souls, from the same gene pool, are led along unique paths.

Finding our path can take some searching, sometimes a great deal of searching. But keep in mind, we are curious by nature, and if we accept this marvelous quality, then the exploration stage — no matter how long it takes — can be the adventure of a lifetime. During this stage we unleash our curiosity and let it take us where we need to be. Curiosity, which has a wisdom all its own, deserves enormous respect: it is a venerable guide.

Theodore Roethke said this well: "We learn by going / Where we need to go." We learn by listening to and following the force that points us. Exploration involves action. No one need teach us how to explore; it's a trait we're born with. We only need to give ourselves permission to do what comes naturally. Releasing your curiosity means allowing yourself to be free. If you let your mind live free, it will teach you much. It will take you to places you never knew existed, some filled with the marvelous, others filled with the miserable. But all with something to teach you.

Exactly how curiosity works is itself a mystery. We don't know exactly why some people hear their callings early in life while others, who look and listen just as hard, do not find their missions until well into adulthood. This largely unexplained phenomenon creates problems in our educational system. As they presently exist, our elementary and secondary schools seek to give students the widest exposure possible to the various academic disciplines. For the majority of young people this arrangement is appropriate. Children should be given the room to explore the greatest amount of territory. But the problem is this: some people know at a young age where they belong, what their mission is, and what they need to get there. They don't need as much time to explore as others do. They hear their callings early.

Our one-size-fits-all educational system has trouble with this. We've concluded that children in elementary and secondary schools are too young to have found their direction. (This myth, by the way, greatly confuses and frustrates youth who believe they have already been led to their life's work.) So we put children who will never need typing or physics or one year of German into those classes, and if they ask why they need them, we give them a condescending lecture that ends with the statement, "Someday you'll thank me."

This kind of education leads children to reject the guidance provided by curiosity. When they are told "We know what's best" by an external authority, they begin to doubt their internal authority. Consequently they can become confused, aimless, and angry. Without respect for their own curiosities, they are lost and will remain lost until they regain this respect. In our culture, if you hear your calling early, your environment may make it difficult for you to heed it.

The amount of patience and tenacity needed during the exploration stage varies. You may have to examine many mountains before knowing which one you are to climb. But then again, your mountain may simply appear before you. Elisabeth Kübler-Ross tells a powerful story that brings this lesson to life:

> I remember a Vietnam veteran who, in the midst of shooting children, pigs, and all moving obstacles in a rice paddy, ordered his gunner to stop shooting. He discovered an old man being given some water by a little girl. As the two frightened people expected to be killed, a great sense of compassion made the American aware of the love between the old man and the little girl. He opened a can of peaches, and they all shared a simple meal together. It was after this incident that the sol-

dier's life was changed, and his story has touched many lives and opened the hearts of some bitter men. This little light within exists in all of us. If we follow it and listen to our inner voices, our lives will be enriched immeasurably.[3]

This soldier had his mountain come to him. He wasn't looking to be moved. Rather, he was, literally, searching to destroy. But even in this killing field that appeared to be ruled by violence and destruction, another message was heard above the gunfire. Just as the bullets destroyed life, this message gave life. This epiphany occurred because the soldier, even in the midst of fear and madness, allowed himself to learn and be moved. At some level he was prepared for an awakening.

Preparing for an awakening is what the exploration phase is about. We can see this clearly in small children. They marvel at many things. Taking a few four-year-olds for a walk can seem endless. They stop and look and touch and wonder at everything. They see things adults never do. Four-year-olds encounter new experiences and objects in a way that seems to say, "Do you have a message for me?"

That childlike, simple curiosity doesn't always directly bear fruit, however. Some people who live lives honest and true to their curiosities struggle to find their missions. They listen and follow but can't recognize where they are being led. It appears to be a wilderness; no one is there, and the place has no name. It can seem as if they have been led to nowhere, as if they have been dumped in a place for people who have no callings. But instead of being people who have been denied a mission, they are, in fact, very special people with a most amazing calling. These are the souls who are called to build brand new roads, roads that may not even have been dreamt of by earlier generations of dreamers. These people are not called to become something that exists; they are called to create something that needs to exist.

Sometimes when you ask people, "What do you want to do with your life?" they may reply, "I don't know." This is actually misleading. People who answer this way may know quite well what they hope to do with their time; they just don't know what to call their project. Established goals like becoming a doctor, lawyer, or police officer are easy to articulate; there are well-traveled roads that lead to those professions. But all those individuals who are called to construct new paths have nothing to call their futures. Unfortunately, we describe these people as confused when they indeed may be extraordinary.

The exploration stage represents a time to look around and get acquainted with life. This stage never really ends. It's just that at some points our curiosities lead us to a focus. Ideally, our curiosities thrive throughout our lives, but as time passes we generally become less like the four-year-olds. We no longer stop to examine every twig and try to interpret each animal sound. Instead, we grow into special interests. Curiosity gradually, at its own pace, becomes selective. It begins to point us in particular directions.

We must keep in mind, though, that curiosity is much more than an intellectual condition. Curiosity is a form of love. It is an intellectual state, but it is also an emotional force. Curiosity is the point where mind and heart become one. When curiosity leads us, it points us toward experiences that the mind wants to know and the heart needs to feel. People too frequently make the terrible mistake of following only their hearts or only their minds. They then end up in a place that leaves them fragmented — feeling betrayed and unsure. Genuine curiosity combines intellect and emotion. Only the force that harmonizes these two dimensions can take you where you need to go.

Some get there quickly. Others spend a good deal of time in the exploration stage. Time spent in this stage can be wonderful. It's a time of learning, experimenting, and marveling. It's a period of wonder and fascination. When elderly people look back on their lives, they often point to these years as the happiest. The exploration stage can be truly a spectacular time, but it can also be a time of anxiety. There is an element of anxiety that comes with not knowing where to focus. Some people thrive on this anxiety. Others crumble.

Those who crumble are those without faith in curiosity. They don't recognize the drive and direction. They see only the indecision. People who have faith in curiosity revel in the search. They accept and love the fact that we are born explorers. And if people around them find their niche first, well no matter. Life is not a race to decide one's fate, and an extended exploration phase hardly makes one inadequate. Visions come in their own time. Some individuals have visions so grand that they need more time to prepare for them. Sometimes you have to grow to a certain height before you can hear your name being called. Time allows you to grow to that height. As the Portuguese proverb advises, "Give time time."

Those without faith in curiosity tend to succumb to the fear. They end their exploration before it's time. They become something safe and convenient. They end their search and then pretend they're happy. They take a job when they should be looking for a life. They marry their neighbor without waiting to meet anyone living outside of their neighborhood. They obey their fear and give no honor to their hearts and minds.

Curiosity is the psychological equivalent (or perhaps the extension) of a guardian angel. It takes you by your core (what some call the soul) and leads you. It is always on your side, as every move it makes serves to educate you. Curiosity is your life force. It draws you to learn more about people. Because it is a form of love, it brings you closer to them as well. But like a good guardian angel, it will take you to places you fear. How else could you grow? How else could you learn where to find courage?

You may have noticed that curiosity acquaints you with fear in gradual doses. This helps you accomplish two important goals. First, you build your courage and increase your internal strength step-by-step. Every child knows it takes a while to build the nerve to get close enough to a squirrel to really see how it acts and what it looks like. In order to reach that point you first study the grass and leaves and then, maybe, the insects. Your curiosity helps you build courage. Second, as this process unfolds you develop a greater faith in your curiosity. It does not ask for total allegiance from day one. It gives you room to develop a relationship with it. Curiosity gives us the time to come to know it.

If curiosity is such a benevolent guide, why aren't more people aware of it? The responsibility for this loss could, I think, be placed at several doors, but the main reason is a lack of mentoring. In our culture we have not been encouraged to seek the wisdom that comes through curiosity. If we were a culture that appreciated the old mentoring the young, the power of curiosity would be no secret. But we aren't, so it is. I will explain this more below, when I address the third stage of calling development.

We need to help people develop faith in their curiosities. Even when the answers don't come immediately, curiosity remains a guiding force. As I have said, some people need to explore for a longer time before they are able to commit and act. Maybe your father really did know in the first grade that he was going to marry your mother and grow up to be a Christmas tree farmer. This doesn't mean you will know so soon. He found his direction in his time. If you are willing to explore, you will find your direction in your time.

You have to be active and patient and courageous. Don't be like the fool in the old story of the man and the lost keys: one night a man out walking his dog happened across a fool on his hands and knees searching for something beneath a porch light. The man called out and asked the fool what was wrong. "I've lost my keys and I'm trying desperately to find them," replied the fool.

"And where did you lose them?" asked the man.

To which the fool pointed off into the distance and said, "Over there, in the vicinity of my car."

Befuddled, the man paused and then wondered aloud, "So why are you looking over here for your keys?"

"Because the light is better," answered the fool.

Exploration routinely involves moving into the darkness, and good explorers are not likely to make impulsive decisions. They examine, consider, and contemplate before committing themselves. One of the signs that the exploration stage may be giving way to the action stage is the growing awareness that you need to act upon what you have learned. You can't study forever without becoming aware that sooner or later you have to face the test. A calling is a call to act, but it does not ask for impulsivity. It requests contemplation prior to movement. As the exploration stage winds down, the things you want to learn are not as important as the things you want to do. It's time to make your contributions.

I need to make it crystal clear that the exploration stage never dies. In healthy people it lives as long as they do. No one is so alive as the person who has a thriving curiosity. Yet there comes a time when exploration moves from the center of one's existence. This is the time when we are called to make our contributions. This is the test, the point where we contribute ourselves. What we contribute is composed, largely, of what we have learned. Learning that does not lead to a contribution to life is not associated with a calling. Useless information, sometimes referred to as trivia, is more of a distraction than anything else. Trivia can certainly be enjoyable. An obsession with it, however, is a way of avoiding that material one really needs to learn.

After the exploration stage flows into the action stage, there may be periods when you need to return. Even the most psychologically and spiritually healthy people get lost now and then. When this occurs, we know two essential facts that lead people back to the place they need to be. First, as discussed earlier, all callings have a universal dimension. Everyone's mission involves a contribution. When we are lost we can begin finding our way by asking ourselves, "What am I to contribute?" Second, we know that curiosity guides us. By returning to the exploration stage we give our curiosities the power they need to direct us. If we keep these two points in mind, we will never be hopelessly lost.

There may also be a third essential fact that can restore our direction. Many people will insist that if you lose touch with your calling you should ask for guidance from the source of the calling. I won't argue with this. But this leads us back to the fundamental mystery we first addressed in chapter 1. Where do callings begin? I believe this is a question individuals must answer for themselves. If you believe that your callings are sent by a force that you can address or dialogue with (such as God), then by all means you should call on that force to help you find your way. But if you think that your callings begin in a source that cannot be addressed (such as your genes), you may not have direct access to the needed advice.

Remember, though, to keep an open mind. You may not know who or what is sending you your calling until you answer it. Even if you are convinced that it is sent by God, you may find that the God you meet by following your calling is quite different from how you conceived of God before you began.

In a lecture to premed students, Abraham Maslow gave this sound advice:

> [The basic] value question is, what vision do you aspire to?...If you really look in the mirror, what kind of person do you want to be? Obviously this doesn't happen by accident. You have to work for it, train for it. If you get a picture of yourself being a good physician, for instance, and of bringing babies into the world, [such a profession can become] a religious experience. Just simply an awe-experience. Well, having that kind of thing means work, very hard work. Medical school is tough. Anything is tough if you want to be good....It's like asking, what do you want to grow into?[4]

I once heard comedian George Burns speak to a group of college students, and he expressed similar sentiments. Specifically, I remember him exhorting the audience to "fall in love with your future!" If you grant yourself the freedom to be guided by your curiosity, you will begin to fall in love with what lies ahead.

The Action Stage

Helen Keller phrased it well, "One can never consent to creep when one feels the impulse to soar." As your path begins to emerge so too does your energy and courage. Although your path will have its challenges, it provides you with the impulse to soar. The exploration stage takes you to the verge of action. It points you in a direction that appears to be yours. You will feel a pull to move that way. Everything seems right.

But, still, that first leap is a big one for everyone. Those who take it tend to have at least one significant quality in common — the willingness to risk. The move from exploration to action is a transition. When there is an attempt at anything there is the possibility of failure. No matter how well you have studied the possibilities, you can't remove the risk.

This transition may be the most important passage in the human experience. I say this because it is the essence of virtually all efforts to inspire. Graduation speeches, inaugural addresses, dedication talks, and other inspirational messages throughout history have included, indeed focused on, the need to act upon our dreams. Inspirational messages, almost without exception, concentrate on this one transition. Those who hope to inspire us to reach the stars and build the best possible world seem to believe that the key is the movement that takes us from dreamers and explorers and moves us to become doers and achievers. It is as if deep inside humankind has always possessed this knowledge, and we try to pass it on every chance we get.

Not long ago a graduate student of mine made an important little point. She said simply, "People love to be inspired." How true. Inspiration is that push to do something that we want to do in spite of the fear. People love to be encouraged. Inspiration addresses the move into the action stage. When you move through fear and follow your dreams, you will find not only courage but also good fortune. Ernest Becker knew this transition well. He insisted that "beyond a given point man is not helped by more 'knowing' but only by living and doing in a partly self-forgetful way." He then went on to quote Goethe as having said that we must plunge into experience. All reflection and no plunging drive us mad; all plunging and no reflection, and we are brutes.[5]

I cannot assure you that once you move into the action stage a beautiful rainbow will appear and sunshine and happiness will surround you. After you muster the determination to act on what you believe is right, life may not become immediately wonderful. Although moving into the action stage is a genuine accomplishment, the gratification is not always immediate. The first steps may be the hardest. English novelist John Galsworthy referred to this when he wrote, "The beginnings...of all human undertakings are untidy."[6] It helps if you're willing to get your hands a little dirty. Dirty hands accomplish a lot. Or, as the Zen saying expresses it, "After enlightenment, the laundry."

As I have said earlier, these beginnings do not always come early in life. Gandhi discovered at fifty his real mission in nonviolent resistance. Cervantes was even older when he began his career as a novelist. And then there was Grandma Moses as well as Colonel Sanders.[7] These exceptional people might be described as the last to know. They began to live their callings at an age when others are arranging their retirements.

The only thing anyone can do to hurry a calling is to listen and look for it with courage and perseverance. We can only control so much here. Before our visions are made known to us, our work is to explore. Thus we have a task even before we know our callings. We look and listen until we find. When we find, we do. We can make ourselves ready to receive our callings. We do not decide when they will be sent.

A former client of mine once explained this in a peculiar way. An attorney in her late thirties, she came to me saying she had been unhappy "for a while." She had two children; she described her marriage as secure, yet her life just wasn't offering the fulfillment she had hoped for. She wanted more from life but didn't know just what. I saw her for a few sessions, and we examined her life. We discussed the past, future, and the here and now. She had a sharp mind and a spirit that was aching to soar. I wasn't sure exactly where we were going with our talks, but I did feel her need to explore her life. So we explored together.

Then one day there came a change. She entered my office, sat down, and said she wanted to tell me a story. She proceeded to tell me that her children were watching cartoons the day before, and she happened to see something that spoke to her.

"The story was about a baby lion who lost her mother," she began with a look in her eyes that told me the cartoon was being replayed in her head. "The baby lion would have starved but a sheep saw her, took pity on her, and decided to raise the small cub with her own young. As time passed it became clear to the young lion that she was different. The lambs were graceful and soft. She was clumsy. But the mother lamb loved her anyway.

"The lion grew and kept getting more and more awkward. She couldn't move the way the others could, and she was not nearly as beautiful as they were. But the mother loved her anyway.

"Then one day a wolf came out of nowhere and seized the mother and dragged her to the top of a hill. The lambs and the young lion watched in horror. They knew the wolf was going to devour her, but there wasn't anything they could do. Then, in that awful moment when all seemed lost, the young lion let out this tremendous roar. Everyone — including the lion herself — was amazed. The wolf froze for a second and then ran for its life."

My client gave me a glance that asked, "Do you understand?" After a moment or two of thoughtful silence she whispered, "Sometimes it takes the worst to teach you what you are." I saw her one more time after this. She politely informed me that she did not need me anymore. I agreed. I've never seen her since. I like to think she found her roar.

Edmund Burke wrote that "the only thing necessary for

evil to exist is for good people to do nothing." When good people suppress their roar, they deny their callings. This hurts. It leads to bitterness and feelings of cowardice. Those who roar feel elation, power, and triumph. The act of doing what's right in spite of the fear is the greatest accomplishment any human can ever experience.

Action involves a decision. No one can make our steps for us. Experiences come along, seemingly out of nowhere, to point us here or there, but these experiences alone will not move us. We choose to empower ourselves. We can also choose not to empower ourselves.

Action leads to courage. As we become more accustomed to moving toward our visions, the movement becomes easier and more enjoyable. Those who continue to move become enthusiastic about life. (Enthusiasm, by the way, comes from the Greek word *entheos,* which means "filled with God.") Enthusiasm fills people with the spirit of movement. This explains the extraordinary level of energy displayed by those who have found their missions. It is as if they possess an endless supply of energy. This energy and movement are what bring people to the source of their callings and what also lead to the mentoring stage.

The Mentoring Stage

A person's life is not complete until she or he has taught something to someone — not just anything, something important. Thus, the last stage of living a calling involves passing it on. This means passing on what we have learned in the previous two stages. It also means passing on the lesson that each of us has our own destiny to fulfill. What we are to teach is a mystery until the time is right. When the spirit is ready, a student appears. Sometimes just one student, sometimes many. Mentoring can be a brief experience, or it can evolve over time. It may involve person-to-person contact, or it may mean lessons written that don't reach another human being until long after one's death.

The quality of a person's life will shape those who come to learn. People devoted to their missions tend to have admirers. For a time one may feel no obligation to teach. But as time passes and one's mortality becomes more and more of a reality, it's no longer enough to be appreciated or respected for one's work. For someone who has lived his or her calling, it is easier to die than to watch that mission end.

In the book *Habits of the Heart*, Robert N. Bellah writes:

> In a calling one gives oneself to learning and practicing activities that in turn define the self and enter into the shape of its character. Committing one's self to becoming a "good" carpenter, craftsman, doctor, scientist, or artist anchors the self within a community practicing carpentry, medicine, or art. It connects the self with those who teach, exemplify, and judge these skills. It ties us to still others whom they serve.[8]

Living your calling means connecting yourself with all of humanity. For that reason those who live their callings never retire. They grow deeper into their visions as they age. They grow into teachers capable of educating others on the methods of their specific callings and, perhaps more importantly, on the importance of finding their own visions and living them with all the courage and loyalty they can muster.

We live in an aging society. In the years ahead greater numbers of people will be living into their seventies, eighties, and nineties. We will be a culture with a greater need to mentor. If the rest of society appreciates this need, we may enter one of the most enlightened eras in history. Today we have lost the concept of "elders." But if we mature out of our youth-is-everything mentality, we may find a great source of wisdom sitting alone and neglected.

If we do become a culture that values its elders and accepts guidance from this special population, we will develop a much deeper understanding and respect for our callings. In a youth-oriented society that does not appreciate its elders, the idea of a calling will be difficult to understand. If you don't listen to the voices that can teach you, how will you ever know? Should our culture grow into a time and place where older citizens are respected as educators, we will also be making it easier for people to move into the mentoring stage. As it is, people can become discouraged late in life and wonder if anyone really cares what they have to say. Unfortunately, this causes too many souls to question and repress their desire to educate. All too often the legacy of knowledge and spirit dies.

A few years ago I met an old man who taught me a lot about all this. I was in the hospital for tests. This was the second time that summer I had been hospitalized. I was thirty-three years old at the time, and for two years I had been having frequent, unexplained fainting spells. The doctors believed there was something wrong with my heart, but after a thousand tests and two hospitalizations no one could find the defect.

On the evening of the sixth day of my hospital stay I met the old man. It was about eight thirty, and all the visitors had gone. Too restless to do much else, I wandered the corridors of the cardiology unit. When I reached the visitors' lounge, I stopped to absorb the view. I was on the ninth floor facing west, staring at a beautiful sunset falling over the city skyline.

I didn't see him at first. Then when I did, it seemed as if he had suddenly appeared. He was right in front of the window, facing the sun, lost in thought. We exchanged quiet hellos and then returned to silence. I wanted to leave him alone, but there was something magical about his presence. We both stared out into the sunset. We both had our cardiac monitors strapped around our necks, and we both had a lot on our minds.

I broke the ice, and the small talk started. He told me he was eighty-four and that the next morning he was to have open-heart surgery. Saying this he went silent again. Before long the conversation picked up once more. I told him I collected Will Rogers memorabilia, and he told me that he used to love to go to the movie theater to watch Rogers's movies. The old man who never said his name then told me that one of the highlights of his life was a phone call he once made to Tom Mix. As the mayor of a small town in Illinois in the 1930s, he was in charge of entertainment for the county fair. He tried to get Tom Mix to come, but Mix wanted seven hundred dollars for the appearance. Too expensive. But a great memory.

At that point my fellow heart patient began to tell me all about his life. He had had a very busy eighty-four years. I guess he was a workaholic who took care of his family and his town. He usually worked several jobs at a time. It didn't seem as if he needed the money that much. He just worked and worked and worked.

The room was dark now. The candlelight that was the sun appeared to flicker for an extra few minutes before it died. All talked out, the man looked down at the floor, shook his head slowly, and started to get up and go back to his room. We shook hands and wished each other well.

As he turned to go I went into a small panic. There was more! I was sure there was more! He had something else to tell me. "Tell me," I asked, trying desperately to find the right words, "what have you learned? In eighty-four years, what have you learned?" Although I felt foolish asking this, he showed no surprise at all. It was as if he had been expecting the question.

He told me that, most of all, people should not rush through their lives. With so many things to experience and people to meet, we should give ourselves time to learn what life is about. He shook his head again and sighed, "We move too fast." Having said this he turned once more to leave. As he walked away he mumbled something under his breath. Barely audible, it sounded as if he said, "Don't miss your days."

"Don't miss your days?" I asked myself in an effort to make sense of it. "Don't miss your days?" I repeated a second time. Then it struck me: *Don't miss your days!* But by the time its meaning reached me, he had disappeared. He left me, however, with a phrase to live with. In the time it takes for the sun to set I had been mentored.

I left the hospital the next day with my heart in great shape. A month later the real cause of my problems would be identified — epilepsy. As I walked down the corridor toward the elevator, I looked into the old man's room. Nurses were changing the sheets. My healthy heart stopped for a moment before I reassured myself that he could still be in surgery, or perhaps he had been moved into another room. I turned and walked toward the nurses' station to ask about his status. After a few steps, though, I was filled with a feeling that said I didn't need to know. I turned around one more time and left the hospital.

The late psychoanalyst Erik H. Erikson once wrote, "Children will not fear life if their elders have integrity enough not to fear death."[9] Those who live a life spent serving an important mission are those with integrity enough not to fear death. They are also the ones who have the most to teach. These souls demonstrate a love for life to those they mentor. It is the love of life that conquers the fear of death.

In order to live this final stage of our callings we must respect what we have learned. Without this respect we will not carry our lessons well. Wisdom, after all, is not so much about the collection of knowledge as much as it is about finding the insights that matter most. Good mentors are not those who pass on everything they have learned; this would take another lifetime. Good mentors are those who have found the essence of things. Good mentors pass on what they need to pass on. It's one of those mysterious coincidences of life that what elders feel they need to teach is usually exactly what their students need. Mentoring brings out the best in people. In the process of mentoring an elder learns what really needs to be taught.

Explorers, Doers, and Educators

Each of the three stages of calling development — exploration, action, and mentoring — may be considered a calling unto itself. Each stage represents a calling within a larger calling. People who live each stage well will build lives for themselves filled with learning, achievement, and significance. They will find courage and direction. They will, of course, encounter difficult times, but if they learn the value of adversity, they will ultimately emerge stronger. For instance, people in their exploration stage who use adversity as a teacher will learn how to survive. People in their action stage who face adversity will learn how to motivate themselves. And mentoring is largely a process of educating folks on how to triumph over life's inevitable adversities.

To be successful in the exploration stage we need to give ourselves and each other room to explore. Curiosity is a natural force that grows as it is allowed expression. It is an honorable guide if we let it be. We do so, first and foremost, by accepting the fact that we need a guide. Getting lost is not a failure; it is a learning experience. In many ways getting lost is a success because it means that we have given ourselves the freedom to wander beyond the safe and familiar. If we allow it, our guide will take us to places we never knew existed.

Success in the action stage means finding inspiration. It means taking the initial inspiration provided to you by your curiosity and then beginning to generate your own. People who live their callings are those who have discovered sources of inspiration. They seek out people, poems, and passages that move them to travel the correct path even when the road gets rocky. They also develop the ability to generate inspiration within themselves so that when no external inspiration can be found, they tap an internal store that motivates them. Inspiration is a fuel that drives people toward their visions. Inspiration comes to individuals in many ways, but it comes most often to those who appreciate its power and look for it.

Inspiration is virtually impossible to contain. It pleads to be shared. Inspired people rarely live secluded lives. Their energy radiates toward others. Just as the curiosity of the exploration stage leads to the inspiration of the action stage, inspiration leads to the desire to share. The desire to share is the essence of the mentoring stage. Curiosity leads to inspiration, and together curiosity and inspiration lead to enlightenment. As it is applied, mentoring grows from desire to love. Those who allow themselves to be mentors eventually find that they love to teach. They also realize all they have to pass on. This realization represents the enlightenment that guides and drives mentoring.

Curiosity, inspiration, and education are the power sources that motivate people to find and live their callings. I am not suggesting that these are the forces that create or send a calling; that wouldn't make much sense. These forces, instead, help us travel the road that someone or something else has built. Like the calling itself, that force will reveal itself to you in its time. We do, however, have what might be an important clue here. In his book _Stride toward Freedom,_ Martin Luther King Jr. wrote a line that has always struck me as very meaningful. He said simply, "The ends are preexistent in the means."[10] What this means for our purposes is that what we will find at the end of our journey already exists in the journey itself.

Then what do we know of this journey? We know at least one critical point. Curiosity, inspiration, and education all have something tremendously important in common. They are all forms of love. They represent the love of learning, the love of life, and the love of helping other people grow. Each stage in the development of a calling is guided by love.

What does this mean? Could it mean that the source of our callings is a loving one? Could it be that this source is with us all along as we move toward it? Could it mean that we are not only sent a calling but are guided by the force that calls us?

More about Rewards

Earlier we began a discussion about the rewards that come to those who follow their visions. We are now in a position to summarize what we know about how callings contribute to the quality of our lives.

But there are certain rewards that go to all those who move toward their visions, blessings collected when one walks the right road. Some of these we have discussed already, yet they bear repeating. And it should be noted that each reward serves to help us continue our mission.

Among the rewards given to those who walk the right road are focus, energy, significance, courage, empowerment, accomplishment, honesty, identity, spirituality, acceptance,

love, and freedom. Although they may come in different se-
quences to different people, they all reach those who have
earned them. Those with the determination to move toward
their visions receive the qualities and the character needed to
accomplish everything their vision asks.

First, a calling is about *focus*. In a world filled with distractions, a calling makes one aspect of life stand out above
all the rest. It pulls and makes a sound that only you can
hear, as if it knew your personal language. It moves you away
from the prison of other people's expectations as you find
your own self-expectation. Focus comes with a triumphant
shout that screams, "This is my life!" A person without focus
is someone who has not yet heard his or her calling. But remember, a calling comes in its own time. Until then it is our
job to learn as much as we can. This learning process is how
we meet our visions. When our visions emerge, we choose
whether or not to move toward them. If we move toward
them, we find our focus getting clearer and stronger and the
distractions falling away.

As our focus becomes stronger, our *energy* increases. It
may be called tenacity, perseverance, determination, or enthusiasm. Whatever its form, energy is one of the clearest
and most accurate indicators that you are on the right track.
When you find your mission, you also find the energy you
need to make it happen. You find the power you need to
make your life's work significant. This is important. Sooner
or later we reach a point where we review what we have
accomplished in our lives. Some of us try hard to keep this
question out of consciousness. Realizing that one has spent
one's life in an endeavor that one does not value can be devastating. To avoid the devastation one may try to avoid the
question. This avoidance, however, requires a great deal of
mental energy, energy that could be spent productively.

Our callings represent the work that makes our lives meaningful to us; that work makes our lives count; it gives our lives *significance*. This means finding what needs to be done and doing it, whether that be as a Girl Scout troop leader or as a stay-at-home father. Your calling is the mission that makes your life significant and meaningful to you. You decide if what you are doing is significant. You live with the consequences.

If you find missions that make your life significant, you will be rewarded with the courage to carry them out. *Courage* then builds as you go. You gather courage as you move toward your vision. First you gain the courage needed to take small risks; as your valor grows you may become almost undaunted by fear. At this point you have made quite a spiritual breakthrough. You have reached the place where your calling is more moving than your fear.

Courage serves as the foundation for personal *empowerment*. Empowerment means taking charge of your life. It's the feeling of being in control of the things that matter most. Empowerment also reflects the confidence that you can live with those flaws and limitations that you cannot erase. It's the understanding that you can have the power in spite of your limitations. You can even be empowered by your limitations because they have so much to teach.

Empowerment is the refusal to allow other people to tell you who you are. It's the release of the defiant power of the human spirit. It is one of the feelings that come with the awareness that you have found your road, your niche, your place. Empowerment is the understanding that you have everything you need to learn how to do the things you need to do.

If you move toward your vision, you will find everything you need to be successful; you will find *accomplishment*. By "success" I mean success in the deepest sense of the word. You may be called to be an elementary school basketball coach. You may work your hardest to be the finest coach you can be. You may never win a single game and yet still be very successful at this calling. Being called to be an elementary school basketball coach may have little or nothing to do with basketball. It may be all about shaping the character of young human beings.

In order to understand success and accomplishment, you have to understand the true nature of your calling. Sometimes it's buried beneath distractions. These distractions often come in the form of pseudofailures. A pseudofailure is an experience that may be thoroughly discouraging until you learn that what you lost is insignificant. Experiences like this can teach us what really matters.

If you follow your callings, you will be successful. You will be triumphant (though often in a quiet way). You will know the victory of being true to yourself. You will know the satisfaction of having contributed to the universe, even if you never win a single basketball game. It won't be an embarrassment that you're not surrounded by trophies. You won't need them. The real successes are the ones you feel deep inside. They occur when you know you've done the right thing. Instead of rewards you may receive criticism. Keep in mind that criticism doesn't necessarily mean you're wrong; it only means that you're doing something that your critics don't want you to do.

If you are true to your calling, you may disappoint a few critics along the way. Following a calling is a journey in *honesty*. Who you are may not be acceptable to some. But with your eyes on your goal you realize that critics are usually only distractions anyway. Living honestly means living with the conviction that you are not going to live anyone else's life. You are honest with the world and honest with yourself. You are committed to what is right and make the contributions you have been asked to make. As you move along the path of your calling, honesty becomes easier and feels more natural.

As this path unfolds and honesty becomes more and more a way of life, your _identity_ becomes clearer. Before you began your search for your calling you may have noticed how other people sometimes try to tell you who you are. Now that you've come close enough to feel its pull, your awareness is redirected. Now you are more aware of what you want to do with your time on earth. This is the point, as President Bush remarked, at which God introduces you to yourself. Your social world no longer defines you. Your spiritual world — your _spirituality_ — is now producing the guidance.

As your identity emerges so does your personal power. You are aware that you have a direction and your own set of standards to measure your progress. You are no longer dependent on the approval of others. You have become a force unto yourself, a force capable of accomplishing great things. I believe in the truth of what Charlotte Davis Kasl wrote in her book _Many Roads, One Journey:_ "Our souls become liberated when we dare to dream, and the happiest, most content and interesting people I know are those who follow their calling."[11]

We reach a breakthrough moment in our lives when we accept our callings. This moment may be a long time coming, but when it does come, we experience a conversion. We can never really accept ourselves until we accept our visions. But when we reach the point where we find peace in our callings (no matter how challenging they may be), we also find a genuine _acceptance_ of ourselves. This acceptance recognizes all the flaws, limitations, and mood swings that come with being human. It's honest self-acceptance without the need for perfection.

Once individuals accept themselves, they can begin to love themselves. Once they accept their callings, they can begin to love their lives. This is one of the essential aspects of the conversion. Acceptance opens the door to love. Since callings lead people to the service of life, one could make a strong argument that the work of a calling is fueled by love. One could also make an equally intelligent argument that callings create their own fuel. People true to their callings are capable of giving love. Their love goes into their work and the people they serve. They share it, and it comes back to them even stronger.

Finally, there is *freedom*. This is actually quite a paradox because it would seem that a calling would restrict one's freedom. After all, if the road chooses you, how can you call yourself free? Well, first of all, anyone can refuse a calling. No one is forced to follow. Even though the echoes of your calling may haunt you, you can build a lifestyle designed to drown out the voices. Many do. But freedom means nothing if you are not able to be true to yourself. Real freedom is about being free *to be you*. It does not mean being able to be and do anything you want. Real freedom means being free to be one thing — who and what you are meant to be. No one is freer than the person who can become who he or she is meant to be. You may never know why you have been given a particular calling. But you will never know true freedom until you allow yourself to be what you have been called to be.

Don't miss your days.

Chapter Five

Hearing Your Calling, Seeing Your Vision, Finding Your Mission

Where there is no vision, the people perish.

— ECCLESIASTES

Learn to get in touch with the silence within yourself and know that everything in this life has a purpose.

— ELISABETH KÜBLER-ROSS

For many people, hearing their calling is a simple, spontaneous experience. Ironically, these folks are sometimes the last to realize that callings exist. Their visions appear so smoothly and without incident that they don't know what a special experience they have been through. They don't hear powerful voices or view overwhelming revelations or encounter breathtaking awakenings. Instead, they move gracefully into the life that they have been called to.

People like this are often born into contexts where they are surrounded by unconditional love. They are loved and accepted no matter which path they take, and if the path they seek does not exist, they are encouraged to *build* the right one. They are encouraged to explore all the places to which their curiosities lead them. In short, they are surrounded by people who, consciously or unconsciously, understand the meaning of a calling.

Then there is a second group, people who also find their callings in a flawless way and yet who do not have the advantages of such a wonderful upbringing. These souls come into the world with an inner ear that is especially sensitive. I think of these people as being spiritually gifted. Even in environments that deny or even ridicule the existence of personal visions, they connect with their visions in an almost elegant style. They rise above a context that tries to pull them down.

Neither psychology nor psychiatry will ever explain spiritual giftedness. There is more to it than these disciplines cover. We may, indeed, never know why some people seem to have a special ear. It is important, however, that we understand that callings have reached people in places that do not appear to welcome callings.

Because spiritually gifted persons move so naturally toward their missions, they too may have a difficult time grasping the meaning of a calling. Their calling and response to it may have been so graceful that those phenomena have gone virtually unnoticed.

Then there is the third group, the rest of us: people who know what it's like to be out of touch with our visions. At the very least, we know what it's like to be unsure if we are where we belong. We have been through periods, sometimes long periods, of doubt. And as if this doubt were not painful enough, it is typically aggravated by the confusion that comes with not knowing how to settle the doubt. It's a doubt with no way out.

All too often people who need direction *wait* for it to come. They think that if they stay lost long enough someone will eventually come looking for them and lead them to certainty. If they wait long enough, though, they become stuck. Then, when no one comes along to rescue them, they become bitter.

I'm sure there are occasions when people who merely wait get rescued. But even in these rare instances there is a cost — time. The clock ticks, and time goes by as the waiting continues. Life is a time-limited affair. The time we lose is gone forever.

There is no single method for reaching one's calling. Rather, there are many ways that lead to this end. We can do more than wait. Those who need to connect or reconnect with their visions or be reassured that they are doing what's right can take an active role in the process. What follows is a list of possible strategies to help people find their missions or reassure themselves that their present path is the right one. This list, however, is only partial: it is but a suggestion of matters to consider. Trust yourself. Your calling is unique. So too may be your road to reaching it.

Consider the Possibility That You Are Already Answering Your Calling

I like to believe that most people, sooner or later, find their missions. Some, however, don't realize what they have. Like the Tin Man, Scarecrow, and Cowardly Lion, they go off seeking advice from others on how to get what they think they need. All the while they are unaware that they already have everything they need.

Don't spend your life searching for something you already have. Before you gaze off into the distance, take a good hard look at what is at hand. We sometimes take for granted the most wonderful things in our lives. Besides this, even when our lives seem nearly perfect, we can get greedy and still want more.

This book was never intended to tell people their callings, but one of its intentions is indeed to help people in finding their true paths. The point at hand is that the right path may already be beneath your feet. If you are unsure or if you feel you have lost touch with your calling, please keep in mind that if an honest, courageous search takes you nowhere other than where you are now, perhaps you are exactly where you are to be.

Follow Your Curiosity

Curiosity is a guide. If you allow it, it will teach you more than anyone or anything ever could. Curiosity is a life force. It is an energy that grows whenever it is given room to grow. If you give it room, it will lead you wisely.

All that you need to know is there waiting for you. But you must be open to it. You have to accept the fact that if you allow yourself to learn new information, you may have to change. People committed to staying the same are incapable of learning. It is those who are open to the changes that learning can bring who are led to where they really belong.

But we can do even better. To be accepting of new information is certainly healthy. The path to your vision, however, becomes even straighter when the openness turns to desire. Desire makes one an active searcher. What was a willingness to learn is now a love of learning. It is the love that removes the fear. You no longer fear what you might become. Now you love what you are becoming.

This process can take time. It may come as a gradual process, or it may come in the form of a sudden explosion. When curiosity bursts to the surface, it can create a crisis in one's life. Although this crisis can be more than beneficial in the long run, to the soul who is not prepared for it, it can be frightening. Take, for example, the oft-discussed "midlife crisis." What is so misunderstood about this phase of life is that this "crisis" is really a frenzy of new questions. During midlife many people are driven by their curiosities to ask new questions, big questions. They want to know if their life has a purpose and if they will be able to contribute anything lasting to the world. They want to know why they were put on this planet and if they are living their lives as well as they can. So many people have a mid-life crisis because it is at this point in life that many people stop repressing their curiosities. When this occurs, there arises an awesome potential for growth.

You don't have to buy or beg for a curiosity. You can never kill your curiosity (although you can repress it long enough and hard enough that you may have to spend a little time getting reacquainted with it). Whenever you feel stuck, consider letting your curiosity guide you. If you give it the freedom, it will give you vitality and direction in return.

Allow Yourself to Feel

If you don't stay in touch with your feelings, you will eventually wind up lost. Following your curiosity will present you with interesting options, all of which may enhance your life. But your head and your heart have to get together. Your feelings help you sort through the alternatives and build a list of priorities. If it's interesting and it feels right, it may be a calling.

Often the simplest and most effective way to help someone get unstuck is to ask them directly, "How do you feel?"

As this question becomes answered, a direction may appear. Feelings are nature's way of getting you involved in life. They keep you from wasting your time as a spectator. The world could not survive with only spectators. Thus the world cannot survive without feelings. Feelings connect you with life. Without them you would drift away from all the experiences that make life meaningful.

Besides, feelings are natural: they come with the body. It doesn't take any work to feel. It does, however, take a great deal of effort to avoid feelings. Not only does this avoidance keep you a spectator, it wastes an enormous amount of energy. Repressing your feelings wastes energy that could be used to benefit your relationships, your work, and your overall quality of life. When feelings are released, so is the energy that repressed them.

Callings require that you touch life. Feelings, more than anything else, keep you close enough to life to touch it, grasp it, and revel in it. It's true that if you allow yourself to feel, you also make yourself vulnerable to fear, hurt, or sorrow. But there are important lessons in hardship. The burden that saddens you most may be the burden that you are here to remedy.

Where Is Your Outrage?

Outrage is a sign. It's a sign that you think and feel something is terribly wrong and needs to change. It looks wrong, feels wrong, and no matter how you try to explain it away, it stays wrong. If you keep yourself from running away from it, you become filled with the conviction that "this can't continue!" With outrage comes a burst of energy. This surge of power gives one the strength to beat the unbeatable foe. It also provides a focus, a challenge that must be met. When power meets focus, people are capable of accomplishing more than they ever dreamed they could.

Yes, outrage is a sign, a sign that you have a mission. If you see the mission yet lack the courage to get started, move closer to the outrage. Let it escalate. Let it build to the point where your soul is so filled with determination that there is no room in your soul for fear. Don't be discouraged if those around you do not share your outrage. They have their own callings. Besides, focusing on them would only be a distraction. Accept your outrage as a sign of what you are being called to do.

Ask Someone You Respect What Your Calling Might Be

Your vision may not appear all at once. It may present itself more like a jigsaw puzzle with different people and experiences filling in the different pieces. Some of us can put our puzzles together without too much help from other people. Most of us, however, could use a little assistance now and then. This need for help is not really a comment on our abilities as much as it is a statement about the complexity of the puzzle. It's not always simple. Asking people whose insight you value can provide pieces that you might otherwise have missed. It will keep you talking and thinking about your mission. These discussions help keep your search alive.

I think we have an intuitive sense about who the people are who can help us with this. The people who can help most are probably those who have done the best job of realizing their own visions. Not only do they have the knowledge, but they can speak the language. They are more likely to know what you are looking for when you ask, "What do you think my calling is?"

Because people rarely ask such a question, it may be a little uncomfortable at first. It's not part of everyday banter. If it weren't for the potential rewards, I wouldn't suggest that you put yourself through it. Like most acts of courage, however, the rewards can be wonderful. As you ask the question, listen carefully, even if you don't immediately agree with what you hear. It may be that you are being given the pieces that you never considered. These may be exactly the pieces you need. If you have the courage to ask and the patience to listen, your puzzle may begin to come together.

Practice Saying, "Maybe I'm Right"

There are times in your life when you need to be able to say "Maybe I'm right." Responding to your vision means emerging from the flock and accepting a mission and an identity that are truly your own. When it is your time to emerge, you don't have to be arrogant: you don't even have to be confident. You just have to act on what you believe to be right. You may move on nervous, shaky legs, but you move. You move because you believe in what you are doing.

Sometimes people sabotage their callings because they are afraid to act. They say they have not found their direction when, in fact, they have found it many times. They resist movement because their signs have not been clear enough to remove every shred of doubt. So they wait. And wait. And wait.

Acting on your calling does not require an endless supply of self-esteem or a ton of assertiveness. It merely requires the willingness to say to yourself, "Maybe I'm right."

"If I Had More Courage, I Would . . ."

Finish this sentence in as many ways as you can. Give your-self a few hours, a few days. Don't give up on it. At first, don't worry if your sentences are illogical or impractical. Just write down all the things that come to mind. When you have finished your list, go back and thoughtfully review your state-ments. Identify the ones that have the most power. They may be the ones that make you the most uncomfortable, or they may be the statements that fill you with determination. In any case, look for the remarks that move you. These are likely to be statements that provide the most insight on where you need to be. As I said earlier, don't let impulse make your deci-sions. No calling asks for that. Let your heart and your head and your need to serve help guide you.

The purpose of this exercise is simple. If fear could not stop you, what would you do with your life? Some people hear their callings but pretend they don't, or they hear their callings but create enough noise and distractions to drown them out. They do this because they fear the mission they are called to. Or they fear the road that leads to their visions. When they stop the noise, the calling returns. So they put more crises (i.e., noises) in their lives in an effort to make the callings go away.

These individuals don't realize that callings provide the courage needed to fulfill them. This does not mean that they erase fear. Rather, they provide the courage to walk through the fear. But in order to receive the courage, you must face the calling.

If you lack the courage needed to take on your mission, don't turn away from it. Look at it! Focus harder on it! See it, hear it, reach for it! The more you focus on it, the more cour-age you will be given. If you refuse to let fear blind you, you are more likely to see your vision. When your vision comes to you, it will bring everything you need to fulfill it. This includes courage. Let fear teach and protect you. Don't let it stop you.

Allow Yourself to Be Afraid

There are people who say they have found strength and character while living with fear. Some have said they found themselves through experiencing fear. Others have claimed to have found God in the midst of being afraid.

Carlos Castañeda wrote, "There is nothing wrong with being afraid. When in fear, you see things in a different way." Castañeda then went on to say that "fear is the first natural enemy a man must overcome on his path to knowledge."[1] A full life will always include an element of fear. In order to live a full life, we have to allow it into our lives.

Connect with Nature

Nature has a voice and a language all its own. No one ever teaches us this language, but we are all born with the ability to learn it. We have to go to the source to learn this language. We have to ask nature to teach us its language.

I don't really believe that nature has a single language. It may speak to each of us in a unique tongue. This would be consistent with the ways of nature. I love Leo Buscaglia's remark that "nature abhors sameness. There have never been two flowers alike. Even two blades of grass are different."[2] This may be nature's first lesson: everything in nature (including each human being) is unique.

If and when someone comes to accept that she or he is unique, the next question is usually: "How am I different or special or unique?" It is at this point that we begin to open ourselves to our individual calling. Nature teaches us how all living things are connected. This fills us with the awareness of our universal calling to contribute to life. Nature, if we let it, also fills us with a desire to know how we are special. It turns us toward the voice that calls us.

Then nature provides the silence that can make it easier to hear a calling. Less noise. Fewer distractions. More simplicity. The fourteenth-century philosopher Meister Eckhart said that "nothing in all creation is so like God as stillness." I wonder if this is because stillness brings you so close to God. If you believe that callings come from God, you may be more likely to hear your message in the stillness of nature. If you are still uncertain about the origin of your callings, nature can be a wonderful place to look for answers.

Nature is the first to tell us that it is _not_ the force that begins a calling. It can do much to help us find our missions, but it does not create our purpose. One of nature's most important lessons is humility. It doesn't pretend to be the highest power. The closer you get to nature, the more you understand that it readily admits its vulnerability. The mightiest oak tree is without a shred of arrogance. Nature, instead, teaches us things that can lead us to a higher power. Many call this higher power God. Nature is honest and humble and does not pretend to be God. If we let it, nature can help teach us to be honest and humble and that it is foolish to pretend that _we_ are God.

Much of what nature has to say comes in paradoxes. The oceans that have been around since the beginning of time are living testimony to the fact that there is so much more to time than the present moment. Yet standing in front of the ocean can overwhelm you with the power and possibilities alive in each day. Standing in the middle of a forest can remind you how immense the universe is and how small you are in comparison. Yet that same moment in the forest can fill you with an awareness of how significant your life can be. It's as if in humility you find your power.

But the most miraculous quality in nature is, I believe, its ability to know what you need to learn. It doesn't burden you with trivia. It speaks to the core of your uncertainty and your mission. It has a way of joining people with their visions. But you have to be willing to spend enough time with it to learn its language.

Solitude

Most callings come in silence. Not even a whisper. Silence. For a lot of us the trick is to find the silence.

Solitude can be the best place to find your answers. Fewer distractions. Fewer noises. Less temptation to hand your decisions over to someone else. Some say that in silence and solitude you find who you really are because here there are no forces that would confuse you or lead you astray. Solitude gives you an opportunity to finish your sentences, speak your thoughts, and dream all your dreams. It also gives you time and permission to listen to all of these.

Yes, solitude can give you time to yourself, for yourself. It has also been suggested that solitude is a "place" where people go to hear God. There are those who teach that God tends to communicate in silence. Mother Teresa, for instance, advised:

> We need to find God, and God cannot be found in noise and restlessness. God is the friend of silence. See how nature — trees, flowers, grass — grow in silence; see the stars, the moon and sun, how they move in silence? The more we receive in silent prayer, the more we can give

in our active life. We need silence to be able to touch souls.[3]

Some people seek solitude to hear the voices of their hearts and souls. Some seek solitude to hear the voice of God. Many go to solitude to seek one and wind up finding the other as well.

While you are entitled to your views on where a calling begins, it seems that those who are at least willing to consider the existence of a higher power may be more likely to find treasure in solitude. Religions have long recognized and taught the power of solitude. Furthermore, they have pointed directly to the connection between solitude and callings. Jesus, Moses, Muhammad, Zoroaster, and the Buddha all sought wilderness experiences to discover major visions.[4] They moved away from the crowd to learn what they needed to know. This method of finding enlightenment is not reserved for saints, prophets, and spiritual leaders. It can benefit all those who respect and accept the wisdom of solitude.

Solitude is a friend to those who invite it into their lives as one would a trusted mentor. In contrast, it has little to offer those who fight it. Start small if you have to: a moment of silence, a few minutes of meditation, a walk by yourself. As you grow comfortable with the quiet, you may hear things you've never heard before.

Learn How to Recover from Failure

Toward the end of his life Thomas Aquinas reportedly remarked, "If I had my life to live over, I would dare to make more mistakes." Failure hurts. But failure also teaches. The most important thing failure can teach you is that you can survive it. It doesn't have to destroy you. You open more doors when you dare to make more mistakes. You learn more, accomplish more, live more.

The fear of failure keeps people from living their lives to the fullest. If you believe that you cannot recover from defeat, you will never risk pursuing your opportunities (no matter how rewarding they could be). Callings do not come with guarantees that assure complete and uninterrupted success. Even when you are traveling the right path you will encounter failure — sometimes the big, really painful kind. When you hit these walls you will be entitled to your hurt. You will also have to decide whether or not to get up and move on.

People with great fear of failure typically imagine that it lurks behind most corners. They don't go anywhere in life because they are convinced that they cannot survive the monsters that are waiting for them. To avoid these beasts they refuse to venture into the unknown. Safety reigns supreme. No risk, no failure...no accomplishment.

Those who understand that they can live through failure are much more likely to achieve their visions. They are courageous in the pursuit of their goals. They are active and strong, optimistic and daring. They dare to dream what may seem like the impossible dream. They think in terms of success because they know that failure doesn't end their mission. It may change the vision, delay it perhaps, but never end it. A Zen aphorism says, "The obstacle is part of the path." Failure is often that obstacle. It can serve to prepare, strengthen, and humble you. The failure may be part of the calling. Sometimes it's the beginning. It's never the end.

Break Patterns

Let's face it, people get stuck in ruts. The ruts are so safe and predictable that they can lure you deeper and deeper almost without your knowing it. Those who disappear in their ruts go through life in a sleepwalk.

Routines give you too much time to daydream. You lose touch with life. Although some routines are inevitable, the more routine you have in your life, the less learning will occur. You begin to learn when you are willing to let go of some of the old. This is an essential part of the exploration stage of calling development. You have to free yourself enough to explore new territories and meet new ideas.

Sometimes it takes only the smallest changes to free those caught in routines. Take a new route to work. Sit in a different seat in class. Change your brand. Talk to yourself in a different language. Walk home. Stop dieting for awhile. Spend more time with your kids. If you are caught in routines, begin your escape with nonthreatening changes. Momentum will build as you feel the freedom. Then the exploration starts. Once the exploration begins, a calling may be heard at any time.

No Referees

Being judgmental is a way to avoid intimacy. People with fears of getting close to others stand at a distance with their measuring devices and evaluate if you are enough of this or enough of that. You'll never measure up to their standards, but the truth is that it's not you who needs to change: it's them.

Being judgmental is also an attempt at control. If I can get you to need my approval, then I control you. You won't go anywhere or do anything without wondering if I approve. You can walk away, but this sense of being controlled stays with you. A referee is like a jailer, and this jail can remain with you wherever you go.

Referees get in the way of your calling. They are distractions that try to shape your life. If you focus on one who insists upon evaluating you, you will miss too much. But the simple fact is that you don't need someone who is always judging you. You need to come to your own decisions. This gives you more self-control, more freedom to find your own way.

Your calling does not come from chronically judgmental people. You have to look elsewhere to find your vision.

Dreams

Dreams don't work for everyone in search of a calling. Further, even those who *are* called through their dreams are not called in all their dreams. Some of their dreams carry important messages; others just carry trivia.

Certain tribes of Native Americans have made a distinction between little dreams and big dreams. The little dreams may result from a bad meal or a difficult day at work. They don't contain much direction. The big dreams, however, do. They bring crucial information and wisdom. They can feel much different from little dreams. They have more power. Sometimes a dream can seem small until you consider it for a time. If its power increases, you may learn that it is a dream with an important message.

The fundamental difference between a little dream and a big dream is its point of origin. Little dreams are rooted in the body or in the psyche. They usually represent psychological issues such as unresolved interpersonal conflicts, fears, or unfinished business. They can also be influenced by biological forces such as medication and illness. Little dreams can, at times, point to problems, and, as such, they can be very important. Still, they don't offer nearly as much as the big dreams. Big dreams arise from the spirit. They offer solutions. They do more than repeat past experiences. They have the capacity to lead us into new places. They start us thinking in a new way or make us begin to question things that we once believed were unquestionable. Big dreams do more than point to trouble. They can teach us. When callings come to us in dreams, they come through big dreams. These dreams feel different, are difficult to forget, and often have a lasting impact.

Find a Mentor

Having a good mentor can be a tremendous asset. Someone older, more experienced, and willing to help you find your way can enrich your life through teaching and listening. Some people have benefited from a series of mentors while others have bonded to a single guide. Either way can work well. Sometimes mentors come along suddenly, almost miraculously. Sometimes you have to go out of your way to find them. Sometimes, sad to say, a good mentor can be very difficult to locate.

If you decide to look for a mentor, there are things you should know. First, look for someone willing to teach you without controlling you. Remember, a good guide will encourage you to find you. Second, find someone who will help you lead yourself. In other words, find someone who won't block your view of God by pretending to be God. Third, look for someone who won't answer all your questions but who will encourage you to face your own unanswered questions. Finally (and this is terribly important), try to find someone who will plant the seeds of mentorship in you so that someday you will be able to pass on the kindness.

Oh, and one more thing: there will be times in your life

when you will need a mentor but will be without one. During these times I would invite you to consider the advice given by psychiatrist Roberto Assagioli. Assagioli recommended that we visualize an old and wise person and then have a dialogue with this wise, old soul. During this dialogue you can ask for guidance. Assagioli believed this technique could be effective because it puts us, in a sense, in touch with the mentor within ourselves.

Give Yourself a Little Room to Be Crazy

Don't accept confinement just because "they" say so. "They" won't live with the guilt and unhappiness that come with an unlived calling. If allowed expression, the human spirit is a vibrant and colorful force that doesn't always color between the lines: it longs to break free of confinement and express itself.

Don Quixote may have been a little nuts, but he personified the beauty of the human spirit. It could be that everyone's vision is an impossible dream that can be reached only by letting loose and charging a bit madly toward the vision. Impossible dreamers have more freedom, love, and faith. The trouble with total sanity is that it can smother the human spirit. This is unfortunate. Because once freed, the human spirit will lift you, love you, and lead you.

Clean Out Your Basement

"Don't let yesterday use up too much of today," Will Rogers once remarked. It's a shame how many people refuse to follow this sound advice. Rogers knew that in order to grow you must be willing to let go.

It doesn't matter that you never got that pony you wanted. Let it go. It doesn't matter that you weren't captain of the football team or prom queen. Let it go. So you didn't get into Harvard. It doesn't matter now. And who cares if you embarrassed yourself a few times along the way? We all have.

Let yesterday be a memory and not an anchor. If you have too many things weighing you down, it will be hard to move ahead. Throw away the bad report cards, the mementos of destructive relationships, and old clothes and beliefs that don't fit anymore. Look one last time at the expectations everyone else placed on you while you were growing up, and then give them to the wind. The wind will know just what to do with them.

Holding on to everything creates a false sense of immortality. It's a way of trying to convince ourselves that things never end. But they do end. And we are better off for understanding this. We don't have forever to fulfill the purpose of our lives. The quality of our lives will not be measured by the amount of clutter we collect. Instead, they will be measured by what we have contributed during our short stay in this world.

Try to Identify Other People's Callings

This is a strategy for beginners, those who are not quite sure of the existence of callings. Looking at other people can be less threatening than looking into ourselves. When you identify someone else's calling, there is no obligation to act. You can stay right where you are.

Trying to understand other people's callings can help you test the reality of callings. While you look, here are some questions you might want to consider: Does this particular person appear to have a calling? Is this person living it or has he or she turned away from it? What do you think this person's calling might be? Remember, this isn't rocket science. The questions are simple and direct. While you are answering these questions and observing, you may learn the language of callings. This process may also build your faith in callings.

Finally, you may find that you are good at recognizing other people's callings. This may be a piece of your own calling. You could be called to help others find their callings.

Write Your Story

There may be themes running through your life that you're not aware of. There may be experiences in your past that become much more meaningful when examined in relation to other, seemingly isolated, experiences. Think of your life as a puzzle. Your experiences create a larger, more coherent picture when they are arranged properly. The picture they create may be what you are being called to.

When you write your autobiography, look for all your meaningful moments — even if you don't understand why they are important. These memories may begin to make more sense when they are viewed as part of a larger picture. Begin as early in life as your memory will allow and pay especially close attention to the early memories. These often contain a great deal of important information.

Most autobiographies are, of course, written in chronological order. They start by describing one's childhood and then move toward the present. While this can be an effective way to proceed, it's not the only method. You may, for instance, find it more helpful to begin in the present and work your way back in time. Or you may write without any time line at all. Just detail your meaningful experiences as they come to mind.

Writing an autobiography of this sort is intended to answer

several key questions. Where are your experiences pointing you? What work has made you feel best about yourself? What were the moments when you felt most in touch with the real you? What work has been most satisfying? A good autobiography looks at both the good times and the bad times. Its purpose is not to judge but to teach. The more you're willing to look at, the more you're likely to learn.

Sometimes you can't see your path until you step outside yourself. Writing and reading your story can give you a new perspective. The process takes your life and turns it into a teacher. This teacher knows you better than anyone else. It speaks your language and knows your secrets. It knows your fantasies, wishes, dreams, and disappointments. It is a teacher that can put together your most important pieces and produce a revelation.

Prayer

Prayer may not make sense to everyone. Consequently, this section is for those who have come to believe that God is the source of their callings. Prayer is how people speak to their Source. People pray in their own way, in their own language, and with their own vision of God.

It seems to be almost human nature to ask God to fulfill our intentions even though at some level we know this is a bit selfish. The Lord's Prayer advises that we focus on God's intentions (i.e., "Thy will be done") rather than our own. This is not easy because to do it we have to give up a certain amount of control, and there is no guarantee we are going to like "thy will." If, however, God is indeed the point where callings begin, then this sort of God-centered prayer is of great importance because it brings us closer to the voice that is calling us. As we get closer, it may be easier to see and hear the work we need to do.

But prayer serves another essential purpose. Prayer leads to humility. While sitting in the presence of the Great Spirit one no longer feels entitled to one's grandiosity. This humility prepares us to accept our calling. Not all of us are really ready for our callings when they come. When we receive our callings, they often seem far beyond our capabilities. They don't usually come with a lightning bolt that provides superhuman strength and removes all fear. Rather, they come with a goal that may seem far beyond our limited skills. Thus, one who prays for a calling may be praying for a mission that may, at first, appear overwhelming. It requires faith and humility to turn over your control and sincerely pray, "Thy will be done."

Many people discriminate against certain callings, but the Higher Power we pray to understands the need for and the value in each personal mission. That Power knows that the world needs carpenters as much as it needs lawyers. It needs artists as much as it needs doctors. And it needs garbage collectors every bit as much as it needs astronauts. Those who pray maturely know that what they receive may not be what they had hoped for. Prayer, therefore, can be a courageous act.

Prayer helps people put into words where they are in their lives. Things are said in prayer that are never spoken anywhere else. People, for instance, who refuse to acknowledge the existence of callings for fear of how such an acknowledgment may sound begin to open themselves to the possibility of a personal vision when they are in the company of God. People see God in different ways and from different perspectives. But I've never met anyone who felt ridiculed when speaking to God about her or his callings.

As people grow closer to God their understanding of God

frequently changes. Earlier I suggested that the God you know when you first find your calling may be quite different from the God you know as you move deeper into your mission. As you move closer to the source you learn more about the source. The picture becomes more complete as you begin not only to see it but to feel it as well.

Some people say that as you move closer to God you become more accepting of God. They say that at some point in your journey toward God you begin to let God be God rather than projecting your own image of the divine. This is another step that involves releasing some control. It means having the faith to accept a God that you cannot control. It means loving a God that you may not completely understand.

I can't help but wonder if at this point a second powerful change takes place. Could it be that when you accept God as God is, you also come to accept yourself as you are? Could it be that this is precisely the point when you are ready to accept and invest yourself fully in your callings? Could this be the point when you stop forcing yourself to be a painter, surgeon, or socialite and accept your true calling?

Meditation

It has been said that you talk to God through prayer and that you listen to God through meditation. Like prayer, there are many forms of meditation. At the core of spiritual meditation, however, is the willingness to listen. This means opening oneself to receive guidance. For meditation to be successful you have to forgo your desire to control what you hear. If you control what you hear, then you are only talking to yourself. If, however, you are capable of receiving new messages, then you are allowing yourself to be guided.

Not all of these messages will be immediately clear. Many

must be carefully thought through before they can be understood. Meditation can be an effective means of finding one's course, but it is not a shortcut. The direct path to truth is often much longer than a shortcut to a pseudotruth. Fortunately, meditation helps one develop patience.

Meditation is an attempt to remove the distractions that keep one from seeing one's mission. To be effective, one must eliminate the noises and biases that keep one from receiving one's direction. Meditation tries to quiet all the human-made demands. This allows one to hear the God-made plans. Meditation is about being in silence. It involves clearing one's mind of the old to create a desire to consider the new. It's not always necessary to be taught meditation by someone else, although there are times when this can help. Many of us have never included any time for meditation in our lives. So, as simple as meditation can be, some people benefit from some basic instruction to help them relax and clear their minds.

It is important to understand that there can be no demands or expectations in meditation. It may be your path to enlightenment, or it may be nothing more than a relaxation technique. You have to accept this from the start. Expectation is an attempt at control. So is demand. When you meditate you release the need for control and open your mind. What comes to you will come in its own form and time.

Write Your Eulogy

When your life is over, how would you like to be remembered? What do you hope other people will learn from your life? After you have thought through these questions, ask yourself if the life you are living has a reasonable chance of producing the legacy that you would like to leave.

A eulogy is a tribute to a life. Some eulogies are filled with memories of a life well lived. They are stories that inspire by reminding others what can be done with a single human life. Eulogies are not about what has died. They are about what will live on.

Write a eulogy that would make you proud of your life. Look at it. What does it say to you? What are the qualities and accomplishments that make you most satisfied? Then, after you have identified the characteristics of a meaningful life (for you), consider how you will develop and achieve these goals. Once you know what you want to accomplish with your life and what you hope to leave behind after your life is through, your energies will be focused. With the focus comes power.

Conclusion

Here is a test to find whether your mission on earth is finished: If you are alive, it isn't.
— RICHARD BACH

Everything on earth has a purpose, and every person a mission. This is the Indian theory of existence.
— MOURNING DOVE [CHRISTINE QUINTASKET]
(1888–1936), Salish Indian

All life has its purposes. Animals are led by instincts that are clear, direct, and nonthreatening. Human beings, however, are called in a particularly human way. Our callings are not always communicated directly; sometimes they come to us through symbols. They often arrive in pieces that we have to integrate in order to grasp their meanings. Then there is the fear of what we may find. We can be called to tasks that appear far beyond our abilities. We can be called to work that will disappoint those whose opinions matter most to us. We can be called to missions that cause us to abandon our existing identity and world.

A calling may come to you in dramatic fashion, or it may enter your life as subtly as a soft breeze. By itself this breeze may not be strong enough to move you. It may not have the might to grab your conscious attention. In order for it to move you to your true path, you must open yourself to it and let it move into your soul. You must look, listen, and feel for it. Finding your calling is not a passive process. You have to look for the signs and the symbols.

While we can deny or avoid our callings, it is important to understand that we do not control them. Earlier I discussed the consequences of refusing our missions as well as the rewards of accepting them. Our purpose in life is to follow our callings. If we do not, we will never utilize our full potential, nor will we move toward the source of our callings. If, however, we accept our tasks and work to fulfill them, we also fulfill the purpose of our lives and, in the process, move toward the force that has designed our purpose.

This can be a difficult process. As a culture we have not truly acknowledged the existence of callings. We have not encouraged each other to find our missions. Some might say this is because there is not enough tangible proof that callings are real. But I don't think this is the most common objection. The existence of callings limits our control. If we had complete control we could choose our destinies in the same way one selects fruit from a produce stand. Callings, however, have a force of their own, a force whose ways we must respect.

This is not accepted well by everyone. In fact, many people in our culture see their most important goal as the acquisition of control. We want to control the moon and the stars, time and tide. This pursuit of complete control is, however, the most foolish ambition humankind has ever created. In our efforts to achieve enormous amounts of control we lose our direction. We will understand our visions only when we stop trying to manipulate them.

We may never know everything about callings. It seems that, for some reason, there is an element of mystery linked to callings. It is as if we are supposed to struggle to find and fulfill them. One might conclude that this mystery makes faith an essential quality in living a vision. Courage appears to be another such quality.

Then there is the question: Why me? This question may have no earthly answer. As human beings we tend to be at least a little egocentric, so it's not surprising that many of us get stuck on this. For now, the best answer we have is: it doesn't really matter. Why you are called to be a clergyman or a Girl Scout troop leader doesn't really matter. What matters is that you find your vision and live it. Why people are given certain callings may be revealed to us in time. For now we have to move with this question still unanswered. If we sit idle until we find the answer, we will miss our days.

Life is not to be missed. We are all called to emerge and contribute in our own special way. The call to emerge is part of our individual calling, and the call to contribute reflects our universal calling. We are each called to be special, and we are each called to sacrifice. Most of us understand the human reluctance to sacrifice. It can be painful. What confuses many of us is how difficult it is for people to accept themselves as special. Emerging from the herd can be frightening. Consequently, having a mission, or a set of missions, that applies only to you can be intimidating. Emerging into your own calling often requires that you walk through fear.

As I have said throughout this book, everyone has a calling. Everyone. But even with faith and courage, a calling can be hard to hear. This may be because you are being called in a language that is new to you. You may even be called by a name that is unfamiliar to you. You are called by name, but it may not be the one you are known by in your social world.

You may have a second name, a spiritual name if you will. It may be the sound of the breeze, or it may be the sound that silence makes for you. It may not be a word or even a sound. It may be a feeling, a symbol, or a sensation that you recognize as you. The force that names you ultimately teaches you that you are an individual whose individuality belongs to the service of life. You are individual, and you are community.

Your success in life comes in neither total control nor in complete freedom. Your accomplishment lies in being dedicated to what you have been called to do. To stay on your true path you must be stronger and more committed than those forces that would distract you from your vision.

I like to think that someday humankind will learn to appreciate callings. When that day comes our world will look different than it does today. All callings will be treated as sacred, and all will receive equal respect. The CEO will walk as a peer with the one called to care for the park. The university chancellor will be humbled by the soul who is called to interpret lectures for deaf students. We will realize that no calling is superior or inferior to any other. We will understand that the call to be a second grade teacher is every bit as hallowed as the call to be a Nobel Prize–winning scientist.

When the day comes that we understand the nature of callings, then we will know that the man who is called to be a farmer has a mission as sacred and essential as those pursued by Lincoln, Dickens, Keller, and Einstein. We will know that the work of the housewife can be as venerable and life-giving as the work of Churchill, Pasteur, King, or Mozart.

There are no small callings. Each of us is called to make a great contribution. Each calling invites us to do wonderful things with our lives. Some visions lead to fame and fortune; others do not. But each calling is equally significant and necessary.

If we listen for our callings and live the missions we have been given, we will receive the power, courage, awareness, and passion to move the mountains that wait for us. All the while we will be moving closer to the force that calls us by name, closer to the force that sends the breeze.

Notes

Chapter One

1. Cited in J. Gallagher, *Voices of Strength and Hope* (Kansas City: Sheed and Ward, 1987), 28.

2. Cited in P. L. Berman, ed., *The Courage of Conviction* (New York: Ballantine Books, 1986), 233.

3. Cited in M. W. Edelman, *The Measure of Our Success* (Boston: Beacon Press, 1992), 70.

4. S. Kopp, *All God's Children Are Lost, but Only a Few Can Play the Piano* (New York: Prentice-Hall, 1991), 105.

5. B. Hoff, *The Tao of Pooh* (New York: Penguin Books, 1982), 40.

6. M. Csikszentmihalyi, *Flow* (New York: HarperPerennial, 1990), 44.

7. D. Viscott, *Risking* (New York: Simon and Schuster, 1977).

8. R. May, *Freedom and Destiny* (New York: W. W. Norton, 1981), 4.

9. H. J. Brown, *Live and Learn and Pass It On* (Nashville: Rutledge Hill Press, 1992).

10. A. Colby and W. Damon, *Some Do Care* (New York: Free Press, 1992).

11. Ibid., 71.

12. V. Frankl, *Man's Search for Meaning* (New York: Simon and Schuster, 1984), 113.

13. Robert J. Furey, *Facing Fear* (New York: Alba House, 1990).

14. Joseph Campbell, *The Power of Myth* (New York: Doubleday, 1988), 71.

Chapter Two

1. Cited in F. D. Horowitz and M. O'Brien, *The Gifted and Talented: Developmental Perspectives* (Washington, D.C.: American Psychological Association, 1985), 9.

2. See ibid.

3. Cited in ibid., 365.

4. Both quotes are cited in H. G. Haas and B. Tamarkin, *The Leader Within* (New York: HarperBusiness, 1992).

5. James MacGregor Burnes, *Leadership* (New York: Harper and Row, 1978), 166.

6. C. G. Jung, "The Development of Personality," in *The Collected Works of C. G. Jung* (Princeton, N.J.: Princeton University Press), vol. 17.

7. C. G. Jung, *Modern Man in Search of a Soul* (New York: Harcourt Brace Jovanovich, 1933).

8. W. James, *The Varieties of Religious Experience* (New York: Mentor, 1958), 31.

9. Ibid., 367.

10. J. B. Watson, *Behaviorism* (Chicago: University of Chicago Press, 1924).

11. R. May, *Man's Search for Himself* (New York: Dell, 1953).

12. A. H. Maslow, *Motivation and Personality* (New York: Harper and Row, 1950), 150.

13. Ibid., 159; emphasis added.

14. E. Hoffman, *The Right to Be Human* (Los Angeles: Jeremy Tarcher, 1988), 256.

15. Ibid., 216.

16. A. H. Maslow, "Fusions of Facts and Values," *American Journal of Psychoanalysis* 23 (1963): 117–81.

17. A. H. Maslow, *Toward a Psychology of Being*, 2d ed. (New York: D. Van Nostrand, 1968).

18. A. H. Maslow, *Religions, Values, and Peak-Experiences* (New York: Penguin Books, 1976), 66, 75.

19. Margaritha Laski, *Ecstasy* (London: Cresset Press, 1961).

20. Maslow, *Toward a Psychology of Being*, 95.

21. Maslow, *Religions*, 59.

22. P. R. Fleischman, *The Healing Spirit* (New York: Paragon House, 1990), 57.

23. Siebert's work is discussed in M. Chellis, *Ordinary Women, Extraordinary Lives* (New York: Viking, 1992).

24. E. Becker, *The Denial of Death* (New York: Free Press, 1973).

25. See ibid.

26. Albert Bandura, "The Psychology of Chance Encounters and Life Paths," *American Psychologist* 37, no. 7 (1982): 747–55.

27. Cited in A. Colby and Damon, *Some Do Care* (New York: Free Press, 1992).

28. Becker, *Denial of Death*.

29. C. Garfield, *Peak Performers* (New York: Avon Books, 1986), 79.

30. Ibid., 106.

31. B. S. Bloom, *Developing Talent in Young People* (New York: Ballantine Books, 1985).

32. D. H. Feldman and L. T. Goldsmith, *Nature's Gambit* (New York: Basic Books, 1986), 123.

33. Colby and W. Damon, *Some Do Care*, xi.

34. The subject is discussed in ibid., 86.

35. D. Shekerjian, *Uncommon Genius* (New York: Penguin Books, 1990), 97.

36. A. Storr, *Solitude* (New York: Free Press, 1988), 17; emphasis added.

37. P. Ferrucci, *Inevitable Grace* (Los Angeles: Jeremy P. Tarcher, 1990).

Chapter Three

1. Cited in E. Hoffman, *The Right to Be Human* (Los Angeles: Jeremy P. Tarcher, 1988).

2. Ibid.

3. J. Campbell, *The Power of Myth* (New York: Doubleday, 1988).

4. C. G. Jung, *Modern Man in Search of a Soul* (New York: Harcourt Brace Jovanovich, 1933).

5. Julian Jaynes, *The Origin of Consciousness in the Breakdown of the Bicameral Mind* (Boston: Houghton Mifflin, 1976), 79.

6. B. Hoff, *The Tao of Pooh* (New York: Penguin Books, 1982), 77.

7. Ibid.

8. E. Becker, *The Denial of Death* (New York: Free Press, 1973).

9. G. G. May, *Simply Sane* (New York: Crossroad, 1993).

Chapter Four

1. R. Assagioli, "Self-Realization and Psychological Disturbances," in S. Grof and C. Grof, eds., *Spiritual Emergency* (Los Angeles: Jeremy P. Tarcher, 1989).

2. In L. B. Smedes, *A Pretty Good Person* (San Francisco: Harper and Row, 1990), 29.

3. Cited in P. L. Berman, ed., *The Courage of Conviction* (New York: Ballantine Books, 1986).

4. Cited in E. Hoffman, *The Right to Be Human* (Los Angeles: Jeremy P. Tarcher, 1988).

5. E. Becker, *The Denial of Death* (New York: Free Press, 1973).

6. J. Galsworthy, *Over the River* (London: William Heineman, 1933).

7. See W. Bridges, *Transitions* (Reading, Mass.: Addison-Wesley, 1980).

8. R. N. Bellah et al., *Habits of the Heart* (New York: Harper and Row, 1985), 69.

9. E. H. Erikson, *Childhood and Society* (New York: W. W. Norton, 1963), 268.

10. Martin Luther King Jr., *Stride toward Freedom* (New York: Harper and Row, 1987).

11. Charlotte Davis Kasl, *Many Roads, One Journey* (New York: HarperPerennial, 1992), 354.

Chapter Five

1. C. Castañeda, *The Teachings of Don Juan: A Yaqui Way of Knowledge* (New York: Pocket Books, 1968).

2. L. Buscaglia, *Love* (New York: Fawcett Crest, 1972).

3. Cited in W. Muller, *Legacy of the Heart* (New York: Simon and Schuster, 1992).

4. R. Andre, *Positive Solitude* (New York: HarperPerennial, 1991).